"Whether your emotions toward your finances are positive, negative, or indifferent, *Money is Emotional* will breathe new life into your relationship with money and leave you feeling strangely excited to create a budget!"

— Heather Rae Hutzel, speaker and bestselling author of
The Book of Life: The Greatest Story Ever Told
HeatherRaeHutzel.com

"Christine Luken's wisdom goes well beyond smart and proven tools for budgeting, improving savings, and reducing debt. She gets to the essence of how money truly impacts everything you do, particularly how you approach and thrive (or not) in your personal relationships. *Money is Emotional* opens up new and fresh ways to make money work for you, not against you. Her writing style is friendly and filled with lots of personal anecdotes, which make her book a great, fast, and informative read!"

— Alan Winters, COO, ProActive Health Solutions
www.Vigoroom.com

I0224835

PRAISE FOR *MONEY IS EMOTIONAL*

"Investing, tax, and other personal finance topics can be complicated and hard to grasp. Christine Luken does a wonderful job taking complex financial topics and making them relatable and easy to understand. Reading *Money is Emotional* is like having a conversation with a knowledgeable friend."

— Robert Pagliarini, CFP, EA, Author of
The Sudden Wealth Solution:
12 Principles to Transform Sudden Wealth Into Lasting Wealth

"Success with money isn't just knowing what to do; it's understanding what holds us back from doing what we know. In *Money is Emotional*, Christine Luken offers practical strategies that can help you achieve and maintain financial success."

— Noah St. John, founder of SuccessClinic.com, Author of
The Book of Afformations®: The Miracle of Positive Self-Talk

"Too often we look at money as a debit and credit issue. We think that if we manage the digits then stress will be alleviated. Maybe... The other aspect is the emotional tie of money. This book will get you well on the way to understanding the power of finances in every aspect of your humanity."

— Brian Tome, Senior Pastor of Crossroads Church, Author of
Five Marks of a Man: The Simple Code that Separates Men from Boys
www.marksofaman.com

"Feeling fear, stress or anxiety around your finances? Christine Luken is here to help you clarify the boundary lines between your money and your emotions so you can make smarter financial decisions. With warmth, empathy, and grace, Christine will serve as your financial lifeguard to keep you from quite literally drowning in your finances. Far too many folks are afraid to wave the white flag when in choppy seas and ask for help in this vital area. Christine's delightful new book will show you why doing exactly this may be one of the best long term investments you can make for your financial future!"

— Manisha Thakor, CFA, CFP, Founder of MoneyZen.com,
Co-author of *Get Financially Naked*

"Christine Luken gives a fresh perspective and honest approach to a highly stressful topic that touches all our lives. *Money is Emotional* taps into the humanity of getting fiscally healthy in a stripped down, realistic and comprehensive way that makes perfect sense. Luken walks her readers through simple strategies to help pave the way for financial well-being. Wonderfully personal and practical."

— Mell Corcoran, Mystery Writer,
Author of the *Series of Shadows*

"Most personal finance books give strategies around spending, saving, and investing, but are less than inspiring. At times it's funny, at times it's serious, but all the way through *Money is Emotional* is, well, human. This book is the perfect combination of money facts, humorous anecdotes, heartfelt stories, and most importantly, fundamental action steps you can implement today to put your financial house in order. Don't delay-read this book now! Then, read it again."

— Brennan Scanlon, Executive Director of BNI Cincinnati, Speaker,
Co-author of *Avoiding the Networking Disconnect*
www.BrennanScanlon.com

"Bad money decisions can haunt a person for years. Wouldn't it be nice to have a proven roadmap to follow to help you get out of the mess you're in? That is exactly what Christine Luken provides in her terrific book, *Money is Emotional*. Christine shares her personal journey out of daily financial stress and chaos and gives you strategies and techniques that everyone can implement to reach financial freedom."

— Dan Bisig, Founder of College and Beyond,
Co-author of *College Entrance Game Plan*

"As an expert on the topic, I know the impact money has on personal stress. Learning to THRIVE with stress and money is influenced by paying attention, being mindful. Christine Luken's book brings the emotional side of money to life. Through the case studies and the practical action items, readers of *Money Is Emotional* will thrive as they apply the lessons to their relationship with money!"

— Dr. Frank Wood, PhD, Teacher, Speaker,
Author and Founder of *Thriving with Stress*
www.yourresilientdivorce.com

MONEY IS EMOTIONAL

Prevent Your Heart from
Hijacking Your Wallet

MONEY IS EMOTIONAL

Prevent Your Heart from
Hijacking Your Wallet

CHRISTINE LUKEN
The Financial Lifeguard

MONEY IS EMOTIONAL
Prevent Your Heart from Hijacking Your Wallet

Copyright © 2017 by Christine Luken

All rights reserved. No part of this publication may be reproduced, stored in a retrieval system, or transmitted by any means—electronic, mechanical, photographic (photocopying), recording, or otherwise—without prior permission in writing from the author.

Printed in the United States of America
ISBN: 978-0-9985912-0-9

All dictionary entries and references, unless otherwise noted, are taken from Dictionary.com, accessed December 27, 2016.

Cover art and manuscript layout by Heather Rae Hutzel at HeatherRaeHutzel.com/AuthorResources

Back cover author photo credit: Amy Oliver
www.photographsbyamyoliver.com

Learn more information at:
www.ChristineLuken.com

Table of Contents

Chapter 63

DEDICATION

To Tom Luzak, My Father:
As my Financial Lifeguard, you taught me the importance of not just throwing others a lifeline, but also teaching them to swim.

ACKNOWLEDGEMENTS

Writing a book is like birthing a baby. The author becomes pregnant with an idea that germinates and grows over time. There comes a point when the idea becomes so large and fully formed it's too painful for the author to *not* birth it in the form of a book. We know that a woman has a team of doctors, nurses, and supportive family members who ensure the successful delivery of her baby. As the author, I can assure you this book was birthed with much painful effort on my part. However, there were many, many people who have cheered me on and ensured a successful delivery of this book. Like a proud mother, I know I will be talking incessantly about my "baby" for a long time to come.

Here are the many people on my book-birthing team who deserve a great big Thank You.

Jesus, my Savior, thank you for lovingly gathering up the broken pieces of my life and using them to bring your Light into the financial darkness of others.

Nick, my husband, thank you for being my soulmate, my rock, and my true partner.

My Mom (Carol Mitchell), thank you for always being my biggest cheerleader and closest confidant.

Nicholle Bays, my best and dearest soul friend, thank you for being my constant companion on this journey called life. I can always count on you to be right there with me, whether in the deep valleys or on the mountain tops.

Heather Hutzel, my sweet friend and fellow author, thank you for creating my stunning cover design, not to mention the assistance with formatting and marketing this book. Mostly, thanks for holding my hand on this rollercoaster ride of writing and publishing my first book!

Cresta Lewis, my editor, thank you for catching the appalling amount of typos and grammatical mistakes before this book went to print.

Dave Ramsey and the Lampo Counselor Training Team, thank you for your continued support and training which started me on the path to becoming the Financial Lifeguard. Special thanks to Les Nienow, Russ Carroll, Chris Hogan, and Lisa Barber.

Nanette Polito and Brennan Scanlon, thank you for being both my business mentors and friends. And thank you to all of my BNI and Acentiv friends, especially my "super fans:" Sandi and Dan Hammons, Glenn and Shelley Warner.

My Beta Readers: Dan Bisig, Erica Ronnebaum, Carrie Cox, Sarah Rader, Heather Hutzel, Carol Mitchell and Tom Luzak, thank you for your invaluable input and support!

My "Dream Team," thank you for helping to spread the buzz about this book far and wide. You are greatly appreciated!

My coaching clients, thank you for allowing me to help you along on your journey to financial health. I am honored and humbled you trust me enough to let me into your vulnerable places so I can help you.

Finally, a big THANK YOU to all of you who supported me in some form or fashion during the writing of this book! There are far too many of you to mention by name, in fact it would fill another book. Please know I am eternally grateful for your friendship and support!

GETTING THE MOST FROM THIS BOOK

Download the free Money is Emotional companion workbook at www.MoneyIsEmotional.com. The workbook has the action items, questions, and exercises mentioned in the book, with space to write out your answers.

I recommend reading *Money Is Emotional* all the way through once, with the workbook at your side. If you are married or otherwise attached, encourage your spouse or partner to read it with you. Take your time reading it, just a few chapters a day. This will give you time to absorb the lessons and put them into practice. Some of you may want to read the book through quickly once, then come back and reread it, taking your time to work through the exercises and action items.

This book is meant to be a resource you revisit when emotional money issues derail your progress to financial health. Come back and reread the chapters that apply to your current money struggles.

Be sure to check out the Recommended Reading List, the Additional Resources, and the 6-Week Money is Emotional Reading Plan found at the end of this book.

I Let My Heart Hijack My Wallet

When I hit financial rock-bottom, four years after graduating from college, I owed money to three different payday lenders. I was behind on my car payment and had past due utility bills and credit cards. Ironically, I was the Accounting Manager for my family's multi-million dollar business, and yet I was bouncing checks at home. Talk about feeling like a hypocrite. How does a smart girl who made the National Honor Society make such stupid mistakes with money? It's because I was making emotional decisions with my personal finances, not logical ones. *I let my heart hijack my wallet.*

From the time I was nineteen, I dated and then eventually became engaged to a guy; we'll call him "Jeff,"[1] who was irresponsible with his money. Unfortunately, many of his bad money habits rubbed off on me. He was in and out of jobs, and in and out of jail. I bailed Jeff out both literally and financially on numerous occasions. Needless to say, the relationship had an unhealthy, co-dependent dynamic. But people do foolish things with money for the sake of love, and I was no exception. It took

---

1. Many names and identifying details have been changed in the stories, examples, and case studies throughout this book to protect identities and maintain client confidentiality.

me seven years to figure out that things were never going to change, so I broke off the engagement and gave the ring back to Jeff (since his mother had cosigned for it).

I clearly remember the breakup. Jeff and I were sitting on a bench facing the pond in our apartment complex, our dog playing nearby. Staring at the pond, I finally gave voice to the truth. "Jeff, I feel like I am swimming across that pond, and you are holding onto my leg. I'm tired of pulling your weight. If I don't kick you off, I am going to drown. Whether you sink or swim, it's up to you now."

Because I had no money and horrible credit due to my bad financial choices, I couldn't get an apartment on my own. Fortunately, my Dad and my stepmom, Francine, were gracious enough to let me live with them rent-free for three months so I could leave the toxic relationship and get back on my feet.

My Dad was truly *my* financial lifeguard. He helped me create a budget and a plan to pay off my debt. I was so stressed out and emotional about my financial mess that I needed an objective person to help me sort out the details. I looked at the department store credit card bill and saw the charge on there for a gift my ex-fiancé had "bought" me. When I realized I was now going to have to pay for it, I was livid. I was mad at him but also angry with myself for allowing him to use the card.

Fortunately, my Dad didn't judge me for my mess; instead, he assisted me in formulating a roadmap to my preferred financial future. He reminded me of the basics of sound financial money management—saving money is good, too much debt is bad, and live within your means. He also taught me the importance of giving to those less fortunate than me. I guess I was feeling a little sorry for myself because after four years of being out on my own in the real world, I had fallen flat on my face. My Dad reminded me that I had food, clothing, shelter and a family who loved me, which made me very fortunate indeed.

I think it's important to add here what my Dad *didn't* do for me. He didn't shield me from the consequences of my mistakes. My Dad and stepmom did not pay off any of my bills, nor did they lend me money to catch them up. You might think it was mean, but it was honestly the best gift they could have given me—a sense of personal responsibility. I needed to feel the pain of my mistakes so I could fix them and learn to avoid going down that road again. My Dad has said to me more than once, "The mistakes you learn the most from are ones that cost you the most."

About a year later, I was driving to work and an amazing thought struck me: *"I can't remember the last time I worried about money!"* It was such a shock to me because I was that person who would lie in bed, balancing my checkbook in my head, trying to figure out if I would have enough money to pay all of the bills. I still had some debt, but I was working my plan and things were steadily improving. That's when I realized there had to be other people out there who were just like I was, living under a heavy burden of money stress and worry. I decided then and there I would find a way to help them get on the road to financial health, too.

I understand that money is emotional, and this book is going to show you how to prevent to your heart from hijacking your wallet. And if your heart has already cleaned out your bank account, I'll show you how to take back control and reverse the financial damage.

PART ONE

The Battle for Your Money Begins in
Your Mind

CHAPTER 1

Thoughts, Words, Emotions

Money is emotional because we humans are emotional creatures, seemingly ruled by our feelings. But when our emotions hijack our wallets, the result is stress and financial chaos. The interesting thing is we have much more control over our emotions than we think we do. We can wrestle control back from our emotions and choose to do positive things with our money. How?

The first step is being *mindful* of our money and the emotions which affect our finances. An alcoholic can't start on the road to recovery until he admits there is a problem that needs to be changed. In the same way, we can't begin the journey to our preferred financial destination until we admit we're not where we want to be right now. You can't fix a problem you refuse to acknowledge.

Emotions—both positive and negative ones—are a reaction to what is going on around us and inside of us. If you're angry, it's because either someone said something you don't like or you're thinking about a situation that's upsetting to you. There's an underlying reason for the emotions we feel. Words—either spoken aloud or thought in your head—precede your emotions.

CASE STUDY: BAIL ME OUT!

The year was 1998. My best friend, Nicholle, came to me with a dilemma. Here's what she said, "Christine… my boyfriend, Ben, is in jail because of a DUI. He called me collect and said he's going to go crazy if I don't post bail for him and get him out of there. The problem is that I'm living paycheck to paycheck and don't have the money to do it. The only possible way I can bail him out is if I cash in the stock certificates my dad bought me for my 21st birthday. Do you think I should do it? Ben's really pressuring me."

My response went something like this, "Are you crazy? Of course not! Don't you dare cash in those stocks your dad bought you for your birthday! Ben's in jail because he chose to be stupid and drive drunk. He's lucky he didn't kill somebody! Ben's getting what he deserves; let him rot in jail for all I care."

She didn't take my advice. What caused Nicholle's emotions to hijack her financial common sense? When Ben said he'd "go crazy" if she didn't post his bail and get him out of jail, Nicholle felt guilty. Even though she didn't have the cash to bail Ben out, she did have something of value that could be converted into cash—the stock certificates from her dad. Nicholle argued with Ben that she wasn't going to sell the stock, but he pressured her by saying, "What's more important to you? Me or money?"

I firmly agree that people are more important than money, but Ben is twisting the truth with his words. If Nicholle had taken some time to reflect on her thoughts and Ben's words before selling the stock, she may have come to a different conclusion. Although Ben was certainly miserable in the county jail, he's unlikely to go crazy from spending a few days in the clink. Ben is responsible for putting himself in that situation in the first place, not Nicholle. By asking her to sell the gift her father gave her for her birthday, Ben is the one who is answering the question, "What's more important to you?" What's more important to Ben is the money that will grant him freedom, not Nicholle. Just because Nicholle initially felt guilt and pressure, it doesn't mean she had to accept it and give into it.

Thoughts form our words and words give birth to our emotions. Our own thoughts and words will directly affect how we feel about our finances and the resulting actions of our money management. When it comes to money, think about what you've been thinking about. What are you saying to yourself—both out loud and in your head—when it comes to money? Are you saying things like this:

- "That's too expensive."
- "I'll never pay off these student loans."
- "Everyone is getting promoted except for me."
- "I'll always have a mortgage."

Here is a startling fact you may not know: the conscious part of our brain only controls 2-4% of our actions! Our nonconscious brain controls the other 96-98% of our behavior. You might find this fact discouraging. "How am I supposed to change my behavior if the conscious part of my brain controls less than 5% of my actions?" you may ask. The good news is you can use your conscious mind to *choose* the thoughts you want to believe and systematically impress them through repetition onto your nonconscious mind.

What's the answer to ridding our brains of negative money thoughts? We can control what we think. The first step is to begin identifying your negative money thoughts. We need to reprogram our nonconscious brains by replacing the negative with positive, productive money thoughts. Look at your list of negative money thoughts and turn them into positives! For example:

- "I can afford to buy the things I need and want."
- "I'm making large payments on my student loans, and they'll be gone in no time."
- "I'm offered raises and promotions at my job."
- "I own my home free and clear."

If you can grasp the power and importance of your thoughts and words when it comes to your money, then positive change is inevitable. Positive thoughts will lead to positive action, which will lead to positive habits. It does take time for these changes to manifest, just as it takes time for an acorn to grow into an oak tree. Repetition is the key to impressing these positive thoughts on your nonconscious mind, which will crowd out and replace the negative thoughts.

ACTION ITEMS

Keep a small notepad handy for several days. Write down any negative statements you think or say about money. After a few days, look over the list and see if you can identify any overarching themes or possible sources of the negative money beliefs you've written down. Rewrite these negative thoughts as positive statements.

(Don't forget to download the free Money is Emotional companion workbook at www.MoneyIsEmotional.com. The workbook has the action items, questions, and exercises mentioned in the book, with space to write out your answers.)

CHAPTER 2

Money Stories

A t times we're not sure why certain financial emotions, thoughts, and actions are plaguing us. They seem to be irrational and we're not sure of their source. All of us have "money stories" from our past, even as far back as our childhood years, which color our present financial behaviors. These money stories usually contain *some* grain of truth and may have served a useful purpose for us in the past. However, when our money stories contain some falsehood or aren't applicable to our current situation, they can harm our financial health. These half-truths about money are typically passed down to us from our parents or other family members.

CASE STUDY: NEVER ENOUGH

Jason grew up as the oldest child of a single mother. His father abandoned his family when he was just 7 years old. At a young age, Jason felt responsible to help care for his mother and two younger sisters. He understood that money was scarce, and he witnessed his mother accepting help from family, church members, and even strangers to feed and clothe them. Fast forward 25 years, and Jason is an extremely successful stock broker. He has purchased a home for his mother and pays many of her bills, with money left over. However, Jason is still fearful of the future and experiences guilt over spending money. His net worth is ten times that of most of his peers, but he is still operating out of his old narrative of "there's never enough money to go around." Jason unconsciously clings to and operates out of his past money story, even though it no longer applies to his current financial reality.

According to Brad Klontz and Rick Kahler, the authors of *Facilitating Financial Health: Tools for Financial Planners, Coaches, and Therapists*, when people find themselves repeating the same painful mistakes around money, there is usually unresolved emotional pain stemming from a past event or relationship. We first need to identify these unproductive money stories and revisit these sometimes painful memories before we can fully embrace a new way of handling our money. When we uncover these narratives and examine them objectively, we can make a proactive decision as to whether they are helping or hindering our journey to financial health. We can then rewrite our money stories to have happy endings.

Here are some common money stories we may be telling ourselves:

- If I had more money, life would be so much better.
- Money is evil.
- I don't deserve more money.
- I deserve to spend all the money I want.
- There will never be enough money. (Common for those who grew up in households that were below or near the poverty level)
- There will always be enough money. (Common for those who grew up in affluent households)
- Money isn't important to me.
- Financial success will make me important.
- Nice people don't talk about money.
- If I'm a good person, God will take care of me.

Left unexamined, these money stories and emotionally charged events of our past can continue to haunt us and harm us, forming impassable road blocks on our journey to financial health. For some, counseling or therapy is beneficial and necessary to heal these emotional wounds. In fact, one of the first things I did when I broke off my engagement with Jeff was to seek counseling. I knew I was operating out of dysfunctional money stories and I needed the help of a counselor to rewrite them with happy endings.

ACTION ITEMS

Do you see yourself, or your parents, in any of these money stories? If so, does a particular money memory that is especially strong come to mind for you? Write it down and consider it objectively. Did this money story fit the past situation? Is it helping or hurting your current financial situation? If you feel overwhelmed by your faulty money stories, consider counseling or pick up the book, *Wired for Wealth: Change the Money Mindsets that Keep You Trapped and Unleash Your Wealth Potential*, by Brad Klontz and Ted Klontz.

CHAPTER 3

Money is Not Evil

One of the most damaging money stories we can cling to is the fallacy of "money is evil." Unfortunately, we may hear messages from family members or in our churches such as, "Money is the root of all evil," and "Blessed are the poor." Too many people cling to this narrative of "money is evil."

Money is neither good nor evil, just as a pen, or any other inanimate object, is neither good nor evil. Money is simply an extension of the person using it. You can take $10,000 and donate it to a homeless shelter. You can also take $10,000 and buy enough explosives to blow up the homeless shelter. The money doesn't choose how it's being spent in the same way a pen doesn't decide what it's going to write on the piece of paper in front of it. *It all depends on whose hand it is in.* The same pen could be used to write a sweet love letter one day and vicious hate mail the next. We don't blame the pen for what's written; rather, we ascribe responsibility to the writer. But how many times have you heard someone say money is evil?

CASE STUDY: RICH PEOPLE ARE EVIL & GREEDY

My ex-fiancé, Jeff, and his family were plagued by the narrative that having money is immoral and rich people are evil and greedy. I remember when Jeff received a promotion at a sales job which meant a company truck. We visited his family for a holiday gathering, driving the truck to go and see them. Rather than congratulate him on his career success, one of his uncles said with a chuckle, "Look at you moving up in the world and getting a company car. Pretty soon you're going to be too good to come and see us here in the trailer park." Even said in a teasing tone, his uncle implied Jeff shouldn't aspire to be more prosperous than the rest of his family. If he were to continue his success, money might corrupt him and he would turn his back on his family. Predictably, Jeff self-sabotaged and lost the job a few months later.

Have you heard the Bible verse, "Money is the root of all evil?" Actually, that's not what the scripture says. The actual wording is "The *love* of money is the root of all evil." (1 Timothy 6:10 KJV) If you are obsessed with money and it's all you think about, you'll be willing to do anything to get it, including hurting other people. This unhealthy preoccupation with money certainly does cause people to compromise their morals in pursuit of it. And here is a revelation: *You don't have to be rich to be in love with money.* In fact, I've met people at all income levels who are obsessed with money and what it can buy. I've also met people at all income levels who have a healthy respect for money, yet are not obsessed by it.

What about, "Blessed are the poor?" Well, that's not what the bible says either. The actual verse reads "Blessed are the poor in spirit." (Matthew 5:3 KJV) Being "poor in spirit" means having an attitude of humility. Another way to say it would be: "blessed are the humble." As you can see, this verse actually has nothing to do with money at all. However, growing up I heard many religious people say, "Blessed are the poor." It was as though they were saying if you were rich, you couldn't be spiritual. Do you glorify poverty? Do you demonize wealth? I can assure you right now, if you believe money is evil and poverty is spiritually superior, you will not be financially healthy.

Money is simply a tool in your hand. If you respect that tool and use it wisely, you'll have good results. If you disrespect money and misuse it, you'll have bad results. If a carpenter does a shoddy job building an addition to your house and it collapses in less than a year, you don't blame the hammer. It's time to stop blaming the only financial tool you have to work with—your money—and time to start respecting it and treating it right.

ACTION ITEMS

Do you believe money is evil and poverty is virtuous? If so, think about the origin of those beliefs. Did someone in your family or at your church pass down this money story to you? Write out a list of ten awesomely generous things you would do if you were wealthy.

CHAPTER 4

Your Relationship with Money

How is your current relationship with your money? Calm and sunny? Stormy and full of drama? Sad and stressful? You may not have thought about it this way before, but we all have a relationship with our money. Whether it is a positive or negative one doesn't depend on how much cash we have, but rather *how we treat our money.*

Think of your relationships in your life right now with your spouse, children, friends, siblings, and parents. What are the keys to successful and happy relationships? Although I'm sure we could enumerate many more, I'm asserting that there are three main keys to a positive relationship with anyone, including your money:

1. Respect
2. Honesty
3. Positive Attention

Respect. If you don't respect your husband or wife, it's going to be nearly impossible to have a good marriage. Disrespect breeds a toxic environment in your home. Your spouse feels devalued and will likely distance himself or herself from you. *Do you respect your money?* If you don't, it will always flee from you! How can you tell if you're disrespecting your money? Here are some signs:

- If you have cash in your wallet, it is disorganized and wadded up.
- You have loose change accumulating in random parts of your house and car and you rarely, if ever, take it to the bank to cash it in.
- You have torn and crumpled receipts all over the place.
- Your bills are disorganized.
- Your wallet is threadbare and falling apart.

How do you begin respecting your money? Ensure your cash is neatly folded in your wallet. When you make a purchase, take the extra few seconds to smooth out your bills and put them back where they belong. Have a designated spot for spare change, preferably in a nice container or piggy bank, and cash it in at the bank regularly. I have a coin purse in my car, which I empty when it starts to get full and a small green piggy bank at home that says "vacation" on the side. Keep both your receipts and bills organized and in a designated spot in your home. I know it seems strange that your money wants to be respected, but it does and it responds positively when you do.

Honesty. It's impossible to have a great marriage when you're lying to your spouse. When you're not honest about your money, you're lying to yourself, which is a dangerous thing. We tell ourselves lies about our money all the time.

- "If I made as much money as my brother, I'd have it made."
- "I'll start saving for retirement when I get my next raise."
- "We NEED a new car because this old one is getting close to 100,000 miles."
- "I'll never be able to afford a vacation."

Here's the truth: every day we are choosing, consciously or unconsciously, how to use our money. Statements like the ones above make us temporarily feel better because we're putting the blame on someone else. We're kicking the proverbial can down the road. We need to be honest with ourselves. No one else can change our relationship with money for the better except for us.

Positive Attention. You can't have a great relationship with your wife if you ignore her and never spend any time with her. This is a no-brainer when it comes to personal relationships. We know if you want a great relationship with someone, you have to spend time with them and give them positive attention. The same is true when it comes to your money. Here are some signs you are neglecting your money.

- You frequently pay bills late.
- You've had multiple overdraft fees within the last six months.
- You don't know how much money is in your various checking, savings, and investment accounts.
- You are perpetually surprised when quarterly or annual bills come around, such as insurance, homeowner's association dues, or car tags.
- Your credit score isn't good and you have multiple blemishes on your credit report.

I was certainly guilty of neglecting to give my money positive attention before I hit financial rock bottom. I wanted to stick my head in the sand because I didn't want to know how bad things were. Guess what? They were bad! And they didn't start to improve until I started spending some concentrated time weekly and monthly with my money. How much positive attention do you give your personal finances on a weekly and monthly basis?

Every week, I take 15 to 30 minutes to balance my three checking accounts (personal checking, bill pay account, and my business account). Once a month, I take some extra time to lay out our budget and briefly discuss anything out of the ordinary with my husband. Once or twice a year, we meet with our financial advisor to discuss our investments. We also have annual conversations with our insurance broker and our tax advisor. A relatively small amount of quality time spent on your personal finances pays big dividends. I promise you, if you ignore your money and don't give it any positive attention, it will *always* flee from you.

Commit to respecting your money and being honest with yourself about your finances. Invest some positive attention into your financial future. Money wants to be managed properly, and once you start doing it, it will grow seemingly like magic. Money problems are rarely about how much you have; rather the problem is your relationship with money.

ACTION ITEMS

Are you respecting your money? Are you being honest with yourself about your current state of financial affairs? Are you spending regular time weekly and monthly managing your money? If you answered "no" to any of the above, what steps will you take this week to make a positive change in your relationship with money?

CHAPTER 5

Money Victim or Victor

A re you a money victim? Do you feel sorry for yourself and the way things have turned out for you financially? Do you say things such as:

- "I'm underpaid at my job."
- "Taxes are too high."
- "Gas/ insurance/ groceries are too expensive."
- "No one can afford that."

If you are blaming something or someone outside of yourself for your money situation, you are in victim mode. I was once very comfortable in my role as a money victim. I recall thinking if I just got a raise, it would solve all of my financial problems. I wasn't ready to admit my part in creating my money messes. I had cast Jeff as the villain in our financial struggles. *He* was the one who wasn't working a steady job and failing to contribute his fair share to our bills. *He* was the irresponsible one who was always asking me for money and expecting me to bail him out of his messes.

During this time, my mom bought me Dr. Phil McGraw's book *Life Strategies: Doing What Works, Doing What Matters.* I remember becoming very angry after reading this sentence: "You teach people how to treat you." I literally threw the book across the room at the wall and started crying. I did *not* teach Jeff to treat me like his personal ATM... Or had I? When he would come to me with a money request, I would first deny it. Then he would keep at it, which would get me upset and argumentative. It would finally reach a point where I would explode, then give in, because I was tired of fighting. Jeff knew if he could weather my emotional storm he would eventually get his way because I hated conflict. My personal boundaries were weak and he knew he could press through them if he persisted.

I didn't pick up Dr. Phil's book for another month after my tearful outburst. But when I did, I was finally ready to receive its truth. I had taught Jeff how to treat me when it came to money and it was *my fault*. As long as I had chosen to remain passive, as a victim, nothing changed. I realized shedding my victimhood meant I could be a money victor, and it was the beginning of the end of that chapter in my life.

As author Joyce Meyer says, "You can be pitiful or you can be powerful, but you can't be both." We won't be able to make positive money changes if we remain in victim mode. It is a painful truth to admit about ourselves. It's easier to blame the current state of our financial affairs on our spouse, kids, employer, or even the government. It's warm and cozy in this cocoon of blame and we can get very comfortable here. I know because I stayed in mine for seven years! It was scary for me to shed my victim identity because I operated under that paradigm for so long. I needed to take personal responsibility for my money messes.

The good news is once I shed the victim cocoon, I could spread my wings and fly. The first stage of emotion that washed over me was regret and sadness because it was my fault my money situation was in its current state. The second stage was a combination of nervousness and excitement over the possibilities. If I wasn't a victim, that meant I had control. If I wanted to, I could choose to change my situation. Was it going to be easy? No. But it was possible. Once I came to this conclusion, I began plotting my actions to move in the right direction.

ACTION ITEMS

Ask yourself, am I a money victim? Am I ready to shed this identity and become a money victor?

CHAPTER 6

The Willpower Myth

Have you tried to fix your money problems through sheer willpower? How did it work out for you? I tried many times in my twenties to rectify my finances through self-control and failed over and over again. My experience is not uncommon. In fact, a survey performed by the American Psychological Association showed that adults ranked "a lack of willpower" as the #1 reason why they hadn't made the lifestyle changes they wanted to.

Willpower can be increased by "exercising" it, but its limits are finite. No person on earth will ever have perfect self-control when it comes to money. Not even me! Interestingly, willpower is drained from multiple sources. Every time you resist temptation-whether it's the temptation to skip your workout, eat a donut, take a shortcut on a work project, or refrain from yelling at your teenager—these all deplete a portion of your daily allotment of self-control. This is the reason why you're much more likely to give into the temptation of eating half a pizza or racking up charges on the credit card after a stressful day.

Many of my clients believe they need a strong dose of daily willpower to succeed with money, but this is a myth. The great news is you only need a very small amount of self-control to set up some powerful habits to ensure your financial success for the long haul.

Willpower is battling a strong and muscular opponent: emotion. Strong money emotions, both positive and negative ones, can cause us to take actions with our money that defy what we know is the "smart thing to do." Interestingly, avoiding negative emotions actually has more force on our behavior than embracing positive ones. For example, a fear of being in poverty can be a more potent driver for workaholism than the desire to be rich. Some of these are born from our money stories which were acquired during childhood, or from a traumatic event in our lives that was somehow entangled with money. If we're going to change our behavior, it's important to examine our thoughts, words, and feelings surrounding money and see if there are any faulty money stories which need to be rewritten.

The other herculean opponent warring with our financial willpower is habit. Habits are seemingly small things, but they have great force in guiding our money toward prosperity or disaster. The dictionary defines a habit as *an acquired behavior pattern regularly followed until it has become almost involuntary*. Financial habits can be our greatest allies or our worst enemies. Good habits are small things that done regularly will yield positive results. If you save 10% of every paycheck, although it seems like a small amount, it will accumulate into a small fortune over time. On the flip side, if you charge $100 more than you make each week to a credit card, in less than five years you'll have racked up over $39,940 in credit card debt (assuming a 16% interest rate).

Habits can be changed, and this does take some effort and willpower to cement these new, healthy habits. Here are some suggestions for implementing positive and lasting money changes:

- **Work on ONE good money habit at a time, so you don't become overwhelmed.** Pick the one that will be the most impactful and focus on it until it becomes ingrained, which will take at least three to six weeks.
- **Automate good financial habits, if possible.** I highly recommend you put saving and investing on autopilot. If you set up recurring automatic transfers from your

paycheck into your savings and 401(k), it only needs to be done once, not every pay period.

- **Link this new habit to an existing one.** For example, let's say the new money habit I want to form is to look at my budget once a week and balance my checkbook. This is going to help me gauge my progress and keep me on track with my goals. I have a favorite show I watch on Sunday nights. I could link this new habit to my TV show. How? I make a deal with myself that I have to balance my checkbook and look at my budget *before* I watch my show. If Sunday afternoon rolls around and I haven't done it yet, I'll be motivated to get this somewhat unpleasant task checked off my list so I can watch my beloved show.

- **Make this habit stick by super-charging it with emotion.** If saving for college is going to allow your son to go to medical school and become a doctor, clearly imagine the day of his graduation. Imagine how proud you will be going to his office and seeing him in his doctor's coat, helping his patients recover their physical health. When you're tempted to skip this month's 529 contribution, the mental image of your son with his stethoscope around his neck will spur you on to save.

By doing all four of these things—working on one habit at a time, automating if possible, linking to an existing habit, and supercharging it with emotion—you'll ensure your new healthy money habit will stick.

ACTION ITEMS

Pick one positive money habit you want to work on this month. How can you automate it or link it to an existing habit? Super charge this good money habit with emotion. For more on building healthy habits, I highly recommend reading or listening to Charles Duhigg's book, *The Power of Habit: Why We Do What We Do in Life and Business.*

CHAPTER 7

The Dream Session

Before you embark on your journey to financial health, you first need to clearly envision your Preferred Financial Future. If you're going to take a road trip to the beach, you have to know which beach you're going to; otherwise you may end up never arriving! Dreams and visions help keep you motivated and enthusiastic about the direction in which you are heading with your money.

Each and every one of my financial coaching clients are tasked with one assignment, and that is conducting a Dream Session. It's an important part of the budgeting process, along with the Reality Check (which we will discuss in a later chapter.) If you're married, be sure to do the Dream Session with your spouse. Set aside two hours when you won't be interrupted by anything and make sure you're both in a positive state of mind. Your Dream Session won't go very well if either of you are tired, cranky, hungry, or stressed out.

The first step is to answer the following question: *"If I woke up tomorrow and felt REALLY good about my financial situation, what does that look like?"* The answer is different for everyone, so don't be surprised if your spouse's answer isn't exactly the same as yours. Here are some answers I hear:

- "Our credit cards are paid in full."

- "We have the cash to go on vacation and not stress out over the cost."
- "Our kids have some money in their college funds."
- "My student loans are paid off."
- "I have the money to pay back the loan from my father-in-law."
- "We have money set aside for emergencies."

In order to flesh out the details of what your Preferred Financial Future looks like, here are some additional questions to ask:

- What do we want to HAVE?
- What do we want to DO?
- Where do we want to GO?
- What do we want to GIVE?
- Who do we want to HELP?

Do not impose any limits on your dreams and goals during this session. Don't worry about how you're going to accomplish them right now. Come up with some dreams and goals you can get excited about achieving, even if they seem impossible. If you're married, listen to your spouse's dreams and goals. You may learn some interesting things about your spouse during the Dream Session.

The second step in the Dream Session is to create your Financial Vision Board. Which dreams excite you and your family the most? A vision board is simply a physical representation and reminder of those dreams. Search the internet and magazines for pictures that represent your dreams. Print or cut out those pictures and put them on a poster board or bulletin board. Hang your vision board where you will see it daily! You can also create a digital vision board by having those same pictures as your wallpaper or screen saver on your computer, tablet, or phone. You may want to consider making both individual and family vision boards. Vision boards can really get your kids to buy into your financial goals. If they know the reason they're not getting pizza delivered for dinner is because the family is saving for a trip to Harry Potter World, the kids are more likely to eat their hot dogs and macaroni and cheese with big smiles on their faces.

Don't limit yourself to a two-dimensional vision board. Some of my goals and visions are in 3-D! For example, when I was writing this book, I created a 3-D representation of it. When I settled on the title of the book, I mocked up a full color book cover. I printed it out and taped it to a random volume from my book shelf. Seeing "my book" on my desk motivated me to keep writing and make this book the reality you are now reading! If there's a certain car you dream of owning, get a miniature version of it and put it where you'll see it daily.

The third and final piece of the Dream Session is to formulate your "Afformations®." You may have heard of "affirmations." Affirmations are statements about your vision being a reality. These are statements such as, "I'm debt free!" "We're paying cash for a Hawaiian vacation." Although this is certainly better than negative self-talk, there is a problem with affirmations. It's the little voice in the back of your head that disagrees with you! When you say, "I'm debt free," the little negative voice replies to you: "No, you're not!" This is why we're going to use "afformations" instead. How are afformations different? Noah St. John explains in his book, *The Book of Afformations®: The Miracle of Positive Self-Talk*, that they ask a *why* question, rather than making a statement, and your subconscious mind searches for a solution.

So, instead of making the statement, "I'm debt free," you would ask yourself, "Why am I debt free?" And instead of saying, "We're paying cash for a Hawaiian vacation," ask, "Why are we paying cash for a Hawaiian vacation?" Did you notice your inner critic is silent when you ask these as questions? Instead of arguing with you, your subconscious mind gets to work on solving the problem. "Hmmm… why am I debt free? Maybe I'm not charging any new purchases. I'm probably paying extra on my credit cards every month. I wonder if I could work some overtime next week…." Suddenly your thoughts are working for you, not against you. I recommend saying your afformations daily, preferably first thing in the morning or last thing at night, out loud.

Be sure to avoid negatives in the wording of your afformations. Here's why: your subconscious mind skips over words like "don't" and "not". For example, avoid saying, "Why don't I have a mortgage?" Instead say, "Why do I own my home free and clear?" Formulate at least one afformation for each of the financial issues you are currently facing and say them out loud daily.

Here are some example afformations to help you get your creative juices going:

- Why is my retirement fully funded?
- Why do we pay off our credit cards in full every month?
- Why do we pay cash for our vehicles?
- Why is my salary $100,000 per year?
- Why are we paying cash for our children's college education?
- Why do I own a successful and profitable business?
- Why do we regularly take tropical vacations?

The best thing about these afformations is that you can use them for all areas of your life, not just for money goals. I have four typewritten pages of afformations for my relationships, health, business, finances, and more. You can't have too many positive afformations!

ACTION ITEMS

Schedule your Dream Session this week. Get started on creating your Financial Vision Board. Write down at least 10 money afformations and commit to speaking them out loud at least once per day. I highly recommend you read or listen to Noah St. John's book, *The Great Little Book of Afformations*.

CHAPTER 8

Your Journey Begins

Now that you have an understanding of why money is emotional and how it affects the way we behave with our finances, you are ready to begin the journey to financial health. It's important to keep your Financial Roadmap handy to guide you on your way.

What is your Financial Roadmap? It's your spending plan (budget) + your savings plan + your debt reduction plan. Planning out your spending each month, minimizing your debt, and maximizing your savings will fast-track your family to financial health.

What is my definition of "Financially Healthy"? In my opinion, someone who is financially healthy has achieved and maintained the following: a positive personal cash flow, an ample emergency fund, minimal consumer debt, and open communication about money with spouse and children. Let's look at each of these in more detail.

- **A Positive Personal Cash Flow.** The only way you're going to have a positive personal cash flow is to spend less money than you bring in on a monthly basis. This means operating with a budget or spending plan. Unfortunately, the word "budget" conjures up visions of wearing a burlap sack, living in a cave, and only shopping at the local dollar store. A spending plan isn't about deprivation; it's about deciding ahead of time how you're going to spend your money, in support of your goals, dreams and visions.

- **An Ample Emergency Fund.** How do I define an "ample" emergency fund? At least six months of your living expenses is a good start. You'll first need to create a budget to figure out how much you're spending every month on your bills and necessities. If you're self-employed, I'd recommend closer to 12 months of expenses in your emergency savings account. This way, when your hot water heater goes out or the inevitable car repairs crop up, you won't have to cash flow these expenses with credit cards.
- **Minimal Consumer Debt.** People typically spend about 15% **more** on purchases charged to a credit card versus paying with cash, or even a debit card. Couple that with high interest rates and it's a serious double whammy to the health of your wallet.
- **Open Communication with your Family.** If you do the above steps and fail to openly communicate with your spouse about money goals and habits, the two of you could be pulling in opposite directions. You should be having money discussions *at least* once a month when reviewing your spending plan for the upcoming month. Couples who regularly talk about money have less conflict and stronger marriages. And don't be shy about having age appropriate money discussions with your kids. It's better for them to learn money basics from you rather than from credit card companies and used car salesmen!

As you start down this road to becoming financially healthy, it's important to know you'll encounter detours and potholes along the way. Just like a cross country car trip, there will be both delightful surprises and disappointing setbacks. As we work through your spending plan, savings plan, and debt reduction plan, I'll point out the emotional potholes that threaten to derail your progress and give you constructive tools to work around them or avoid them all together.

Are you ready to start moving towards your Preferred Financial Destination? Let's go!

PART TWO

The Budget: Your Key to Financial
Health

CHAPTER 9

Taming the Money Monster

When our financial lives are in disarray, we feel stressed out and anxious. Many times we're scared to see just how bad the situation really is. Money can be like a monster under the bed. It paralyzes us and keeps us awake at night. We walk through our days with this undercurrent of dread about our finances. We're afraid to face the truth about our finances and do our best to ignore it.

In a recent study, 72% of people responded that they are always or sometimes stressed about money. Interestingly enough, 68% of Americans do not have a monthly written spending plan. *Why don't more people do a monthly budget?* I think it's because they're afraid to look at the details. Ignoring money problems only makes them worse, just as ignoring a health issue doesn't make it go away. If you had horrible headaches several times a week, would you avoid the doctor because you were afraid it was a brain tumor? That sounds a little silly, doesn't it? But many people avoid looking at the details of their finances because they are afraid of what they will find. Doing a budget tames the imagined "Money Monster" because you bring it out into the light and deal with it. We can't fix a problem we refuse to acknowledge.

We know stress takes a toll on us physically. When we are stressed about money, it can cause a host of health issues. Stress raises the risk for heart attack and stroke. It causes us to lose sleep at night. Stress can lead to poor food choices, which can increase the number on the scale. Before I hit financial rock bottom more than 15 years ago, I would lie in bed at night, trying to balance my checkbook in my head. "My paycheck is deposited tomorrow morning. Hopefully, the check I wrote on Wednesday hasn't cleared yet. Will I have enough grocery and gas money left after I pay bills?" No wonder I was having trouble sleeping!

I didn't realize how much money stress ruled my life until I was out from under it. On top of health concerns, I'm sure it's no surprise to you that money fights are the #1 cause for divorce. Financial stress can cause a downward spiral, not just in our wallets, but in our families and in our physical bodies.

Here's the good news: you can stop the downward spiral right now. When you begin to be mindful about managing your money, your peace will increase along with your bottom line. Budgeting with your spouse or partner has been proven to decrease money fights because you're now communicating about what's important to you. Does this sound too good to be true? I promise you, formulating a monthly spending plan will improve your relationship, your bottom line, and your well-being. I've coached countless people over the past decade and have witnessed firsthand this transformation in my clients who take it and run with it.

The solution for taming the out-of-control "Money Monster" is to pull it out into the light and examine it up close and personal. I promise it's not as bad as it seems. Gathering all of your financial information and tallying up your monthly payments and your balances seems scary, but the best way to tame the Money Monster is to get it out of your head and onto paper!

If you don't know what you're dealing with, you can't make a plan of action to improve your situation. Instead, you walk around with this vague sense of fear and anxiety, which accomplishes nothing other than stressing you out. Sometimes we need to get to the point where the pain of staying the same is worse than the pain of changing.

ACTION ITEMS

On a scale of 1 to 10, with 10 being "extremely stressed" and 1 being "not at all stressed," how would you rank your current money stress? Are you ready to pull the Money Monster out into the light?

CHAPTER 10

The Reality Check

Imagine you are planning a road trip to the beach. You have the luggage, your family, and your dog packed into the car for a week of fun. You pull out of the driveway and immediately have a decision to make: Do you turn right or left? Once you get on the highway, are you going north or south? East or west? Some of these decisions will be based on which beach you're going to. My route from Cincinnati to Myrtle Beach will be very different than my route to Miami Beach. This seems like common sense, right?

However, it's shocking how few people put the same amount of time and effort into planning their financial journey as they do their summer vacation. Many people are "driving around," hopelessly lost financially, because they've failed to take an honest look at where they are right now and where they want to go. We've already talked about the importance of the Dream Session and determining your Preferred Financial Future. Now it's time for the other half of the equation: the starting point. A few days after you've completed the Dream Session, it's time for the Reality Check.

In order to create a Financial Roadmap, you need to know your starting point, not just your destination. If you are part of a couple, you must involve your spouse or partner in this process. Chances are, if you are not living on a budget right now, you don't really know what you're spending monthly on things like gas, groceries, and entertainment. Gather your bank and credit card statements so you can see your spending history. I want you and your spouse to approach the Reality Check like detectives or archeologists on a discovery mission. In fact, you can even pretend you are looking at someone else's financial records. Your objective here is to record and report the facts, not to judge your spending—or each other. So, tread lightly here.

It's time to get financially naked! This means coming clean about any secret credit cards or hidden savings accounts. The Reality Check can turn into a yelling match if you are not careful. Before you begin, determine to put your energy into moving forward, rather than blaming each other for past mistakes. Even single people can fall into the trap of beating themselves up for their financial transgressions, which doesn't solve any problems. Now here is the big question: *Is your current spending in line with your values, dreams, and goals?*

CASE STUDY: EATING OUR SAVINGS

Several years ago, I had a coaching session with my friend "Jenny." She was frustrated because she felt like she should be saving more money for the future. Jenny told me that her husband made good money, and there's no reason they shouldn't have a fully funded emergency fund. I began looking over her monthly expenses and discussing them with her. I noticed Jenny had a big, fat zero on her budget sheet in the Dining Out category.

"You never eat out?" I asked. "No, my husband and I rarely go out to eat," she said. I noticed several pizza boxes on her kitchen counter. "How often do you order pizza delivery?" "Once a week, on Fridays. That's pizza night," Jenny replied. "And how much do you usually spend?" "Well, since we have four kids, it's usually close to $50 with the tip." "Ahhh…I see. And do you ever drive through McDonald's?"

I'm sure you can figure out how the conversation went from there. Jenny discovered that her mindless spending on pizza and fast food was keeping her from meeting her family's savings goals. When she saw the "Dining Out" category on the budget, she thought of nice dinners at sit-down restaurants, not fast food and pizza delivery. We were able to make a plan to cut back—not eliminate—her dining out expenses, so my friend and her family could have fun while still saving for the future. Therefore, be prepared to encounter some similar surprises during your Reality Check.

~

Schedule your Reality Check for a time when you'll be calm, focused, and uninterrupted. Most people need about two hours to complete the Reality Check.

Here are the items you will need for the Reality Check:

- Monthly Household Bills: Mortgage/Rent Payment, Utilities (Electric, Cell Phone, Water, Cable), Car Insurance
- Credit Card Statements: Monthly Minimums and Payoffs
- Other Debt Payments: Car Payments, Medical Bills, Home Equity Line of Credit, Student Loans. Monthly Minimums and Payoffs for all.
- Amounts Spent Monthly on: Gas, Groceries, Dining Out, Entertainment, Pet Care, Health & Beauty, Kid's School Supplies and Activities, etc.
- Pen/pencil and paper, or your laptop. Write down what you have been spending per month for all of the categories above. (You may have additional spending categories not included in the list.) Total up the amount of debt you currently owe.

During your Reality Check meeting, please abide by these guidelines:

- Discover; don't judge! Pretend you are a private eye investigating someone else's personal finances if you must.

- No yelling. It shuts down the communication process and accomplishes nothing. Determine to put your energy into moving forward, not blaming each other for past mistakes.
- Come clean. If you are hiding debt or savings from your partner, admit it.

Now that you have completed the Reality Check, ask yourself: *Is my current spending in line with my values, dreams, and goals?* You might discover that your mindless spending on unimportant things is keeping you from your Preferred Financial Destination. Taking responsibility for your current money situation isn't easy. It's painful to face the truth about ourselves. We frequently feel embarrassed or ashamed of our situation and it makes us hesitant to ask for help. I had an accounting degree, and was working as the Manager of Accounting for a multi-million dollar company when I hit financial rock bottom. Talk about feeling like a hypocrite!

If the Reality Check is emotional and unproductive, it's likely because you and your spouse are *not* on the same page. It may be helpful to have an objective third party help you through the budgeting and debt reduction process. My Dad did this for me. Every time I looked at my bills, I felt upset and angry. There was a story behind each of those debts and how they came to be. I was mad at my ex-fiancé for not contributing toward the bills he helped me run up. My Dad was able to take the emotion out of the budgeting process for me. He helped me logically lay out a plan to pay everything off. Once I had the initial budget laid out for me, it reduced my negative emotions because I now had a plan with specific tasks and goals. You may want to seek the help of a financial coach or counselor (or even a family member or friend who is financially savvy) to assist you with your first budget.

ACTION ITEM

Schedule your Reality Check within the week!

CHAPTER 11

A Budget is Not a Diet

Unfortunately, when most of us hear the word "budget," we cringe. It conjures up images of deprivation, discipline, and going without. We imagine that budgeting is the equivalent of a crash diet of celery and water. However, a budget is really more comparable to a healthy eating plan, rather than a diet. There is room for portion-controlled fun in our budgets!

Budgeting is simply planning out our spending monthly before it happens. If the word "budget" makes you feel icky, call it your "spending plan," "financial freedom plan," or "money wellness plan." The budget is the most important part of your Financial Roadmap because, without it, it's nearly impossible to pay down debt and systematically build up your savings. You need to have a handle on your monthly cash flow first.

Have you tried to follow a diet with very strict eating rules, such as "no desserts allowed" or "no fried foods *ever*?" How long did you stick to it? A week? A few days? A few hours? I tried a multitude of diets to lose those "last 15 pounds." Guess what? None of them worked. It wasn't until I found a healthy eating plan which allowed me the liberty of having occasional treats, like a piece of birthday cake, that I lost those pounds and have kept them off. In the same way, if your budget has *zero* fun built into it, you're going to fall off the wagon sooner rather than later. The good news is there's room for portion-controlled, but not unlimited, fun in your budget!

In the book *Happy Money: The Science of Happier Spending*, by Elizabeth Dunn and Michael Norton, the authors discuss how placing limits on our financial fun actually makes us *happier*. We enjoy the little pleasures in life, like massages, Belgian chocolate, and fancy lattes *more* when we have them less often. You've heard the saying, "familiarity breeds contempt." When we have unlimited access to these types of treats, they cease to be treats and become part of our routines. Many people get into financial trouble because they haven't put reasonable limits on their spending. Maybe that's why you've picked up this book. Oftentimes people become very confused about their needs versus their wants. "But I need my latte!" you say. While it may be true that you need your caffeine fix daily (as I do), homebrewed coffee will do the trick as well as a $5 latte. Going without a coveted treat for a period of time actually leads to increased levels of happiness when we finally do get it. Coffee drinkers rated their happiness levels higher when they consumed a latte once a week versus every day. People reported more satisfaction with a monthly massage than weekly ones.

What treats have you allowed to turn into routine experiences? By placing reasonable limits on them, we can return them to their treat status. The result is increased happiness while saving money. This saved money will be put to good use, helping us achieve our Vision Board goals. Please resist the temptation to cut out your treats altogether (unless you are in a negative cash flow situation, being hounded by bill collectors). This will only put you in "financial diet" mode, which usually results in a gallon-of-ice-cream-like shopping binge.

ACTION ITEMS

What has been my past experience with budgeting and how do I feel about it? What do I hope will be different this time? What is my motivation to be more mindful about my spending? What treats have turned into routine expenditures for me? How will I adjust their frequency to return them to treat status?

CHAPTER 12

No Cookie Cutter Budgets

W e are unique and our budgets should reflect that. You're not going to find a hard and fast set of budget rules in this book because I don't believe in "cookie cutter budgets." Instead, I'm going to give you a framework of guidelines, tips, and best practices you can customize to fit your particular situation. Some of you reading this right now are married with two or three kids, others of you are single and just starting your careers, and still others of you are approaching retirement. I'm not going to give you an exact budget to use; instead, I'm going to teach you to budget for *yourself* and your particular situation.

~

Since you've completed both your Dream Session and your Reality Check, it's time to formulate your first spending plan for the upcoming month. I usually do my budget the Saturday before the next month begins. What happens if it's time to do your first budget and it's the middle of the month? Go ahead and do your first budget for those two weeks, and then your next budget will be for the entire following month. This is a great way to dip your toes into the budgeting process and get some extra practice.

When you schedule your first Budget Session, pick a time when your brain will be fresh and you'll have no distractions. If you have kids, this might mean getting a babysitter or sending them to Grandma's house! Your spouse or partner must also be present with you at the Budget Session. If you're single, you may want to enlist the help of a financially savvy friend, family member, or mentor to assist you with your first Budget Session. Here is the one rule I'm asking you to keep for this monthly meeting; respectful discussion only, please. Nothing gets accomplished when you yell.

Using your Reality Check as a starting point, allocate every dollar of monthly income to a category: expenses, saving, debt reduction, and giving. Unless you're single, it's usually not just one person in the household handling 100% of the money. If you are part of a couple, decide which of you will be responsible for each category. For example, I take care of the groceries, clothing, and entertainment categories and my husband is responsible for gas, auto, and home repairs. Divide these expenses up in a way that makes sense for you and your family. There is no right or wrong way to do this.

One mistake my clients frequently make is forgetting about things that are paid for once a quarter or once a year. So be sure to set aside money *this month* for variable expenses which will be paid out in future months. For example, you may pay your car insurance quarterly instead of monthly. I still want you to earmark the money every month for the car insurance, even though you're only paying the bill every three months. And if you usually spend $600 on Christmas presents every December, begin setting aside $50 per month so the cash is available when you need it. You can move this money over to a savings account if you think you'll be tempted to spend it.

Expect to make midcourse corrections to your spending plan during the month. Your budget is not carved into a stone tablet, never to be changed. Rather, it is a flexible tool that changes with your financial reality over the weeks, months, and years. It takes 60 to 90 days to forge a new habit. Your first budget will have numerous changes. Your second budget will have changes, but not as many as your first one. The longer you budget, the easier it becomes. It will take less time and you'll have fewer changes and corrections, so be patient.

Budgeting is very much like wakeboarding: you face plant numerous times when you first start! If you've never heard of wakeboarding, it's very similar to snowboarding, but you're on the water being pulled by a boat. My husband and I owned a boat for ten years. For the first two or three years we had it, I tried to wakeboard multiple times, but couldn't get up on the water. It may have been that I was trying to use my husband's board (which was way too big for me) or it may have been bad technique on my part. One summer, I borrowed my sister-in-law, Amber's, wakeboard and took some pointers from her, and I finally popped the board on top of the water! I can't adequately explain the exhilaration I felt speeding across the water—until I hit a small wave on the surface, lost my balance, and face planted. Honestly, I fell more times than I'd like to admit during my first summer of wakeboarding. And sometimes it hurt fiercely, but I kept at it. It felt like 90% pain and struggle, and only 10% fun at first. However, the last year we owned our boat, I was experiencing 98% fun and only 2% pain and struggle. Budgeting is very much like wakeboarding. Expect a few face plants early on. And when they happen, get up and shake it off, and get right back at it.

Your first budgeting session will likely be the most difficult and stressful. Each month, the meetings will take less time and effort. The only additional piece to future budget sessions will be the post-mortem budget examination. *Before* you formulate next month's budget, take a few minutes to examine the past month's budget versus your actual spending. What worked out well this past month? In which budget categories did your family over or underspend on, and why? Did you forget to plan for a certain expense? What could you have done better? What changes can you make going forward to ensure those budget blunders can be avoided?

Let's say you forgot about your Identity Theft Protection insurance policy renewal this month. You pay it annually and it costs $240. How could you prevent this expense from sneaking up on you in the future? You could set up an annual alarm on

48

your phone to remind you a month before the policy renews. This way you'll know before your monthly budget session occurs that you need to add it to your expenses. You may decide it would be less stressful just to switch it to $20 monthly installments instead of one annual payment. Maybe your family also overspent the budget on groceries last month. You may elect to switch the grocery budget category to cash instead of credit or debit to help you be more mindful of your spending this month.

~

Here are some common questions my financial coaching clients ask me regarding their spending plans:

Which budget format is right for me? The answer is the one you will use consistently! If you are tech savvy, there are numerous budget apps and websites to make tracking your spending a breeze. I use my bank's online budget program which automatically pulls in the activity from all my accounts and categorizes the transactions. I can quickly see how my spending stacks up against my budgeted amounts with a few clicks. I even get emails when I'm getting close to the limit on certain budget categories! If your online banking program doesn't have a budget module, you can get the same functionality for free with websites like Mint.com. Other options would be budget worksheets or spreadsheets you use on your computer, or even good old pen and paper. Choose the format that will be comfortable and easy to use. (If you would like the budget forms I use with my coaching clients, you can download them for free at ChristineLuken.com/financiallifeguard)

How do I know if the amount I am budgeting for a certain category is reasonable? The Recommended Percentages for Budget Categories is a measuring stick to see if your expenses are reasonable. If you're off by 1 or 2% one way or the other, there's probably no need to worry. However, if your car payment is 40% of your take home pay, Houston, we have a problem!

Recommended Percentages for Budget Categories

Charity 10–15%
Savings 10–15%
Housing 25-35%
Utilities 5–10%
Food 5–15%
Auto Expenses 10–15%
Clothing 2–7 %
Healthcare 5–10%
Personal Care 5–10%
Fun 5–10%
Debts–Goal is 0%

What if I spend more than I'm supposed to in a certain budget category? Keep in mind that no one does this perfectly. If you spent too much in one category, see if you can reduce your spending in another area to make up for it. You *will* need to make changes to your budget during the month. So, use a pencil if your budget's on paper. The longer you budget, the easier it will be for you.

ACTION ITEM

Schedule and conduct your first Budget Session.

CHAPTER 13

More Bills Than Money

"**W**hat should I do if there's not enough money to pay all of the bills?" If you're asking this question right now, there's no doubt your money situation is *very* emotional and stressful. I know, because I've experienced this for myself. When I hit financial rock bottom, I was behind on my car payment with bill collectors calling and threatening to repossess it, past due on most of my other bills, and owed money to three different payday lenders.

When bill collectors come calling, we experience a range of unpleasant emotions. We may feel guilty that we're not able to take care of our family financially. We might feel ashamed because we're behind with our creditors. We could be panicking about ruining our good credit score. When we are in this downward emotional spiral, there's a higher probability of making a bad situation worse.

~

I have the unique perspective of personally experiencing both sides of the collections world. For three years, I worked part-time for a national bank in their collections division. It wasn't a glamorous or exciting job, but the schedule worked with my college classes and it had the added benefit of tuition reimbursement. As I worked my way up the ranks, finally into a position that collected from customers who were 90 days past due, I learned a great deal about collection tactics.

There were very specific things my coworkers and I said in order to "encourage" card holders to bring their accounts current. Of course, everything the bank told us to say or do was perfectly legal. However, they intricately understood the emotional hot buttons to press with their customers to increase the likelihood of payment. Our job was to collect as much past due money on each account as quickly as possible. Sometimes we would pretend to care and befriend the people we were calling in order to get a commitment to pay. Other times we would remind them sternly of the dire consequences to their credit and the possibility of wage garnishment to scare them into compliance. We were trained to use emotion to the bank's advantage. It's important you understand this when you're dealing with bill collectors.

The interesting thing is there was a short period of time while I was still working for the bank when I was also on the *receiving* end of the collection calls. I always paid that bank's credit card on time or else I could lose my job. (Imagine the irony of me working in the 90-day past due department while having a co-worker call me at work from the 30-day past due department to collect on my credit card!) Shortly after graduating from college, I was able to find an accounting job in a more pleasant environment. However, collectors were still hounding me.

I distinctly remember the local bank calling me regarding my car loan. I was 45 days past due and the collector told me if I didn't make a payment within the week, a tow truck would be sent to repossess my vehicle. "Imagine how embarrassing it will be to have your neighbors see your car towed away," he said. A shot of adrenaline went through me and my blood turned to ice. If I had no car, I couldn't work. And if I didn't work, I wouldn't get paid, and the downward spiral would continue. For a week, I parked my car in a different part of my apartment's complex, backing it in so the license plate number wasn't easily readable. Then I would walk a good half mile to my apartment. I was scared. I felt like a phony and a criminal.

If you arc in a collections situation right now, or know someone who is, I want to give you the tools to take control over your state of affairs from a place of deliberate calm, not fear and panic. Yes, you do owe money and it is your responsibility to make good on your obligations. However, I want you to make a plan ahead of time, before the collectors start calling, so they don't bully you into a money move that could be detrimental to your long-term financial health.

~

What *should* you do if there's not enough money to pay all the bills and collectors come calling? This is the financial equivalent of a medical emergency! There's no time to waste—action needs to be taken immediately, because your financial health is on the line. The first step is to write out your budget if you haven't already done so. This will tell you if you truly don't have enough income to cover all of your basic needs, or if you are just mindlessly spending money on unnecessary things. There is much confusion over needs versus wants these days. Cable with HBO, Showtime, and NFL Season Pass is a *want*, not a need. If you are behind on your credit card bills, you're going to have to cut the cable. It's time to slash all expenses down to the bare bones so we can rectify our situation.

The second thing you need to do is take care of the necessities. By necessities I mean: food, housing, transportation, and clothing. It's important to make sure these needs are met *first*, so you are in a better frame of mind to deal with bill collectors.

Buy food before you pay any other bill. Food means basic groceries, not filet mignon, or dining out at restaurants! Yes, you are probably going to be eating beans and rice and Ramen noodles while you work to get yourself out of collections.

Your next priority is to make your house payment or rent. If you are worried about eviction or foreclosure, you are going to be very emotional and make poor financial decisions. Also be sure to pay your basic utilities, such as the electric and water bill. It's likely you'll need to downgrade your cell phone plan or cancel your cable to help make up the shortfall of funds in your budget.

Once your food and shelter are taken care of, transportation comes next. Set aside gas money and make your car and insurance payment. If your car payment is more than 10 to 15% of your take home pay, you may need to make a plan to sell it and get something more reasonable. If you have access to public transportation, it may be a good solution for you in the short term.

Most people have enough clothing and shoes to get them through a tough spot. However, if your child's shoes are falling apart, please buy them a new, reasonably-priced pair before you pay your Visa bill.

It's most important to take care of your basic needs first. *Do not* go hungry trying to protect your credit score! Bill collectors may try to bully you into paying them more than you can afford by threatening to ruin your credit score or garnish your paycheck. Their job is to collect as much money as they can on each account, as quickly as possible. This is why it's important to have a plan and stick to it!

Now that we have taken care of our necessities, it's time to divide what is left proportionally to our other bills. Be sure to pay something on every debt you owe, even it's just $5.00. Let's say your monthly minimum due payments on your debts total $600—but you only have $300 after your basic needs are met. Since you only have 50% of the total, you will pay half of the minimum due on each account.

Don't dodge collector calls and leave them uninformed of your situation. Communicate with them on a regular basis, but stick to your plan. They will likely not be happy with your reduced payment, but if you send them *something* every month, it is rare they'll make a move to garnish your wages or seize your bank account balance if you are making regular payments.

It's important to mention that this is a short term, temporary plan. You must take steps *now* to rectify your negative cash flow situation by increasing your income, cutting expenses, or likely both. When someone comes to me in a collections situation, they frequently ask me if they should file for bankruptcy. In my experience, most people are able to take the steps to improve their financial health and avoid bankruptcy court. In all the years I've been doing financial coaching, I have only recommended two people file bankruptcy. So, the good news is you are *probably not* bankrupt! However, it is going to take some sacrifice and concentrated effort to resuscitate your financial health.

If you have already cut all of the fat out of your budget and still cannot make ends meet, there is no shame in consulting with an attorney to see if bankruptcy is an option for you. It's important for you continue to learn about sound financial management even as you are going through the bankruptcy process because you want to ensure you don't repeat the same money mistakes of your past.

ACTION ITEMS

Have you ever been in a position of not having enough money to cover all of the bills? If so, how did you handle it? Is there someone you know who could use this information right now? If so, please share it with them!

CHAPTER 14

Mindful vs. Mindless Spending

According to Psychology Today, "Mindfulness is a state of active, open attention on the present. When you're mindful, you observe your thoughts and feelings from a distance, without judging them." In other words, being mindful means *paying attention* to and evaluating your words, thoughts, emotions, and actions.

For many of us, our daily money transactions are on autopilot and we give them little to no attention. We sail through the drive thru and pick up our $5 mocha latte grande every weekday without questioning if that's really how we want to spend $1,300 of our annual income. I'm not saying you shouldn't treat yourself to fancy coffee; it's just that most people have never stopped to think about all the little mindless daily transactions which affect their personal bottom lines. We seem to understand the concept of mindless eating and how it can rack up empty calories which expand our waistlines. The same thing applies to mindless spending that accumulates on credit cards and shackles us with worry over large monthly payments.

I recently coached a newly divorced single dad with a son in high school. This man's now ex-wife was a high-powered corporate executive and had always managed the family's finances. He was simultaneously dealing with a large cut in his income plus a lack of experience when it came to money management. He was completely disconnected from the mechanics of his money, and it was a source of embarrassment for him.

This man came to me in a panic because he was constantly "robbing Peter to pay Paul" and didn't know how to reverse the downward spiral. We worked through his budget numbers and did the reality check of what he was spending on the various categories. When we calculated how much he spent on groceries and dining out each month, we were both in shock—over $1,200 for two people! He said it never seemed like he was spending much, just $10 on lunch and $35 on a dinner out... but when you're buying groceries and letting them spoil in the fridge because you don't know how to cook, the cost snowballs fast!

Mindful Money Management, at its core, is paying attention to our thoughts, words, and emotions when it comes to personal finance, and then consciously choosing the actions which will move us towards our Preferred Financial Destination. Let's think of our journey to financial health as a road trip. Emotions have the potential to be potholes that jar us or even damage our vehicles. If we look down the road ahead and see those potholes before we drive over them, we can proactively maneuver around them, saving ourselves both stress and money.

So how can we shift ourselves from mindless spending to *mindful* spending?

Again, we can find a solution when we look at the tools people use to become mindful eaters. Many nutritionists recommend three tools for doing this: keeping a food journal, measuring out portions, and pausing before and even during eating to assess one's level of hunger. Thankfully, there's a money equivalent for all three tools to help you become a mindful spender.

1. **Keep a small notebook with you for a week and record every penny you spend.** The act of writing down each expenditure takes you off of autopilot and makes you aware of your spending. Just as keeping a food diary will effortlessly cut your calories, keeping a spending log will make you think twice about everything you buy.

2. **Portion out your spending money as cash every pay period.** Dieticians ask their clients to use measuring cups and portion out their food because people become disconnected from what a portion size really looks like. We can also become disconnected from our money and what we're really spending when we're solely using credit and debit cards. We may set a monthly limit of $200 for entertainment, but we lose track of how much we've actually spent halfway through the month. By portioning out your spending money as cash, it is right there in your wallet and you know *exactly* how much you have left to spend.

3. **Pause and take a deep breath before you head to the register or online shopping cart with your purchase.** Ask yourself these questions: Do I need this? Do I really want this? Will this truly bring me enjoyment—and for how long? Do I have the cash to pay for it? How am I feeling right now? By pausing and questioning your spending motives, you may uncover that you're shopping to relieve stress or because you're lonely, not because you really need or want the thing you're about to buy.

These three tools, especially when used in tandem will quickly shift you from mindless spending to mindful spending. The benefits of this will be saving money, fewer instances of buyer's remorse, and peace of mind. For my coaching client, I recommended he begin planning his meals with easy recipes he and his son could cook together. I also suggested setting firm budget limits, using cash for both groceries and dining out, and pausing to think twice about all of his spending activities.

ACTION ITEM

Which tools discussed in this chapter will you begin to use this week to shift yourself into a state of mindful spending?

CHAPTER 15

When Is It Okay to Splurge?

Sometimes we get so entrenched in the mindset of paying down debt and saving money that we struggle with figuring out when it's okay to loosen up a little and enjoy some of our money. There is definitely a right way and wrong way to splurge so you don't ruin your financial health.

When I help people create a roadmap to get to their Preferred Financial Destination, one of the things I discuss with them is pace. I'll ask them: "How fast do you want to get there?" Certainly, I want my clients to be financially healthy as soon as possible, but these things don't happen overnight. I have clients who are very fired up about being debt free and they are eager to sprint to the finish line. I have other clients who want to travel this journey at a more moderate, but constant pace, "power walking" towards financial health.

One thing I have seen with individuals who want to sprint is they can be in danger of burning out. I recommend they take a one-month break two or three times a year, and use some of their money to splurge on themselves. The journey to financial wellness is a marathon. I've had clients attempt to sprint too long without a break, never splurging on themselves and end up falling off the wagon. This is why it is important to treat yourself and your family *occasionally*, even while you are in the process of saving money and paying down debt. Let's first discuss when it is *not* okay to splurge!

- It's *not* okay to splurge if you are in foreclosure on your house, behind on your rent or car payment, or past due on any of your bills. Your financial health is in grave danger, and your top priority should be rectifying your negative cash flow and cutting all unnecessary expenses so you can bring your bills current.
- It's *not* okay to splurge if you don't have the cash to pay for it. Never charge your splurges on a credit card (unless you have the cash to pay it off in full at the end of the month) or put a vacation on a home equity line! This is why many folks are in debt in the first place.
- It's *not* okay to splurge if you don't at least have a small emergency fund, preferably one month or more of your household expenses. This is your financial safety net and should be your top priority, even above paying extra on your debt.

If you have a small emergency fund, you're current on your bills, and you have the cash saved up for a splurge, what else do you need to consider before you treat yourself?

Ask yourself, "Will this purchase bring me joy? If so, for how long?" If you're going to briefly put your financial freedom plan on hold, make sure you are going to thoroughly enjoy your splurge and not regret it later. Dr. Thomas Gilovich, a psychology professor at Cornell University who has been studying the question of money and happiness for more than two decades, has discovered something interesting. Over time, people's satisfaction with the things they purchased went down, whereas their satisfaction with experiences they spent money on went up. Gilovich says you'll get more happiness spending money on experiences like going to art exhibits, doing outdoor activities, learning a new skill, or traveling with your friends or family than you will with the latest gadget or a newer car.

CASE STUDY: DAD'S MILESTONE BIRTHDAY TRIP

My brother, Jim, and I recently took my Dad on a golf vacation to the Greenbrier Resort in West Virginia for his 70th birthday. We started planning this trip more than a year before it took place, so Jim and I had plenty of time to set aside the money we needed for my Dad's birthday trip. We played golf on the nation's oldest course with old fashioned hickory sticks. We shot sporting clays at the Greenbrier Gun Club. We enjoyed room service and decadent dinners out. I even took a falconry lesson, and then enjoyed a special spa treatment while my Dad and brother played 18 holes on a PGA championship golf course. Yes, it was an expensive splurge, but one that all of us thoroughly enjoyed because it was a fun and meaningful time we shared together. I'm sure our satisfaction with our Greenbrier vacation will only increase over the years, sharing the photos and stories of our adventures together.

If you decide to splurge on a thing instead of an experience, make sure this splurge is something you will either use frequently or will last you for many years—preferably both. I'd rather see my client spend her money on a piece of jewelry she'll wear often and have for years than a trendy pair of shoes that will be out of style next year. One way to evaluate this is to consider the cost per use of something. For example, let's say Liz spends $500 on a pair of trendy shoes she wears 20 times over the next year before they're out of style. The cost per use of those shoes is $25 per wear. Now if Liz instead spent $2,500 (cash she has saved) on a pair of diamond earrings and she wears them at least once a week—say 50 times per year—for the next 15 years, her cost per wear is only $3.33. And Liz will likely have those diamond earrings for more than 15 years! Crunch the numbers to ensure your splurge is worth it.

Other tips to implement when splurging:

- **Plan your splurges in advance** so you have adequate time to save up the cash to pay for them. Set goals for the things and experiences you most want to splurge on and be creative about making and saving money to pay for them.

- **Shop around before you buy**. The more patience you have, the more likely you will be to find a better deal.
- **Consider the opportunity cost** of your splurge. If you spend $1,000 on a vacation, it means you can't use the money to pay off credit card debt. What are you missing out on if you do that? If your credit card rate is 16%, this means you'll be paying an extra $160 in interest this year by spending the money on a vacation instead of paying down the credit card. The vacation is actually costing you not $1,000, but $1,160. I'm not saying you *shouldn't* take the vacation, I'm just saying to be *mindful* of what you are forfeiting when you choose one option over the other.

I do want you to splurge occasionally while you're on your journey to your Preferred Financial Destination. If you follow the above guidelines when you do splurge, you'll thoroughly enjoy the money you spend and won't be plagued with buyer's remorse.

ACTION ITEMS

Decide on the pace you are comfortable with as you go on your journey to financial health. Are you a sprinter, power walker, or something in between? Decide how often you are going to build in splurge breaks on your journey. I suggest once every four to six months. What things or experiences do you want to save for your splurge?

CHAPTER 16

The Income Rollercoaster

If your income varies from month to month, budgeting can be a seemingly impossible task. Realtors, entrepreneurs, commissioned salespeople, and other small business owners face unique money challenges when some or all of their household income varies from month to month. When business is great, life's a party, and we're booking a cruise to the Bahamas. When sales are down, we're eating Ramen noodles and dodging collector calls.

I've had coaching clients tell me, "I can't do a monthly budget because I have no idea what my income is going to be!" The truth is those with variable income desperately need a budget so they can smooth out the highs and lows and get off the income rollercoaster.

Budgeting with variable income has some extra steps to it, but it isn't complicated. The first thing you need to do is clearly understand your family's personal monthly expenses. How much does it take to pay your basic household bills every month? Look at the history over the last six months to a year from your bank statements and credit card bills.

Unlike those folks with a steady monthly income, your spending plan will have two parts: the Base Budget and the Overflow List. The Base Budget includes everything that *must* be paid in a given month: house payment/rent, car payments, gas, utilities, basic groceries, minimum due payments on credit cards, etc. The Base Budget will tell you how much money you need to bring in at a minimum each month and it gives you a baseline income goal. If you are fortunate enough to have a spouse with steady income, as I do, your Base Budget can be established on the amount of income you *know* will be coming in, no matter what.

The Overflow List is your "wish list" of the items you want to take care of, if your variable income is greater than your Base Budget total. You would include things like vacation, paying extra on debt, adding money to the savings account, entertainment, etc. (Even if you don't have variable income, the Overflow List is a great tool to pre-plan how to wisely spend a bonus, tax refund, or other windfall.) There are two ways you can handle your Overflow List. You can write out the items with set dollar amounts for each one, or you can assign a percentage to each item on the list, with them totaling 100%. If your income is above your Base Budget for the month, you'll already have a plan for the extra income. The Overflow List will show you exactly where the money will go. And some of it definitely needs to go into your "Personal Sweep Account."

~

Many businesses have a line of credit or sweep account with their banks. Essentially, a sweep account ensures the main business checking account has a steady balance in it. If the account dips below this predetermined balance, the sweep account adds money to pump the value back up. If the checking account starts to get "fat," it sweeps money away, paying down the line of credit.

It's a smart idea for anyone who has variable income to maintain a *Personal Sweep Account*. This is different and separate from an emergency fund. (I advise all of my coaching clients to have six to twelve months of living expenses in their emergency fund.) A personal sweep account is different because you are either pulling from it or depositing to it every month in an effort to maintain a steady standard of living and smooth out those harrowing highs and lows.

It does take a measure of discipline to establish the personal sweep account, because you must purposely fund it in your prosperous months so it's available to pull from in the lean months. How do you calculate the ideal amount to keep in your sweep account? Let the past be your teacher by studying your cash flow history. What was the worst stretch of bad months you've had in a row over the last two to three years? How many months last year did you bring in less than necessary to cover your family's living expenses (your Base Budget amount)? How much would the total shortfall be if all those months happened in a row? Answering these questions will give you a good feel for an appropriate amount to have in reserve. And don't forget, if you pull from your sweep account this month, you'll need to replenish it with your next prosperous month!

CASE STUDY: VARIABLE INCOME

Jennifer and Todd were always stressed out about money due to the erratic nature of Todd's self-employment income. Jennifer works part-time at her children's school and brings home $1,500 per month. Todd owns a landscaping and snow removal business and his take home pay varies widely throughout the year. Jennifer and Todd have completed their base budget and know they need to have $4,000 per month to take care of the household bills.

Their annual take-home income is about $63,000 per year, much more than the $48,000 they need for the base budget. However, here is how their monthly cash flow looked last year:

Jan–$5,000
Feb–$7,000
Mar–$2,000
April–$5,000
May–$8,000
June–$7,000
July–$7,000
Aug–$8,000

Sept–$6,000
Oct–$3,000
Nov–$2,000
Dec–$3,000

It would be nice if they had their $63,000 divided equally by 12 months and had $5,250 in monthly cash flow, but you can see that's not the case. There are four months in which Jennifer and Todd are bringing home less than $4,000 (March, October, November, and December.) If all of those months happened to occur right in a row, they would face a $6,000 shortfall. This $6,000 number becomes Jennifer and Todd's goal for their Personal Sweep Account. In their "fat" summer months, they need to systematically set aside money so it's fully funded before October. In the past, they would cash flow the shortfall on a credit card and pay 16% interest on it until they could pay it off the following year.

Budgeting with variable income can be a bit more challenging than budgeting with a steady salary, but it's definitely doable! Yes, it does take some time, effort, and self-discipline to set up and maintain a Personal Sweep Account, along with your Base Budget and Overflow List. The payoff is removing yourself from the emotional and financial rollercoaster that many people with variable income ride each and every month.

ACTION ITEMS

Do you have variable income due to commissions, self-employment, or bonuses? If so, take the time to formulate your Base Budget, Over Flow List, and the goal amount for your Personal Sweep Account.

CHAPTER 17

Turn on the Cash Flow

We've talked a great deal about controlling your spending, but this is only half of the budgeting equation. If your family is still struggling to reach your Preferred Financial Destination after trimming unnecessary expenses, the problem may be a lack of income. Don't get me wrong—for most people, the problem is out-of-control spending, not how much money they make. If you never master your monthly expenses, it won't matter how much money you earn because *you will spend it all!* That being said, once your spending plan is in place, extra income can be fuel in your tank to propel you toward your savings and debt reduction goals.

There are plenty of ways to turn on the cash flow, and I'm going to give you a bunch of them! Certainly there's at least two or three you can utilize to put some muscle behind your financial goals.

Make More Money at Your Current Job. As financial expert Dave Ramsey so eloquently puts it, "There's a great place to go when you're broke: *to work!*" You may have some opportunities to make more cash with your employer. Here are some ideas:

- Work some overtime before or after your shift, or on the weekends.

- Ask for a raise, but be prepared to demonstrate to your boss how you have contributed to making the organization more successful.
- Apply for other jobs within the company with more pay and responsibility.
- Ask your boss if there are any additional duties you could assume in your current position which would warrant a raise.
- Take advantage of training or classes available through the company to take your skills to the next pay level.

Get an Additional Part-Time Job. You can make some serious cash working a few evenings or on weekends to help make a dent in your household bills. Here are some part-time jobs almost anyone can do:

- Park cars
- Wait tables
- Deliver pizzas or Sunday papers
- Work as a cashier at a local retail store
- Bartend

Monetize a Hobby or Skill. Most of us have skills and hobbies that other people would be willing to pay us to do for them:

- Babysitting
- Pet Sitting / Dog Walking
- Lawn Maintenance / Landscaping
- Party Planning
- Photography / Videography
- Cooking / Baking
- Cleaning
- Organizing
- Minor Home Repairs
- Auto Maintenance
- Painting

- Shopping
- Running Errands
- Tutoring
- Sewing
- Interior Decorating
- Carpentry/Woodworking
- Music Lessons
- Teaching a Language

Buying & Selling Stuff. If you're a collector of anything—from antique china to Star Wars figurines—you probably have a good idea of what fellow collectors are looking for and what they're willing to spend. Consider buying when you find a great deal—even if you don't want the items for yourself—and resell them. Here are a few ideas from people who do just that:

- Buy designer label clothes in good condition from thrift stores and sell them on eBay (size doesn't matter, because you're not keeping the clothes for yourself!)
- Scour yard sales and garage sales for gently used sporting equipment, like golf clubs and bowling balls. Clean it all up and consign the items at a used sporting goods store.
- Hit up estate sales and auctions and bid on antiques or other items for which you have expertise, and resell them at the local antique mall.
- Find ugly furniture to refinish, reupholster, or paint. Then resell is as "shabby chic."
- Buy gently used toys and baby items, clean them up, and resell them on Craigslist.

Freelancing. If you are a writer like me, or a social media maven, you can make some extra money helping small businesses who need writing, marketing, or other technical assistance. What's better than making money from home, sitting in your sweatpants? Some possibilities include:

- Copywriting / Editing
- Social Media Management
- Writing Articles and Blogging
- Web Design
- Virtual Assistant

Join a Direct Sales Organization. Plenty of people make serious cash selling a product they already use and believe in through a direct sales organization. Essentially, you make money because there's no storefront, overhead, or chain of distribution companies, like regular retail establishments. Be sure to do your homework first and find out what it costs to start, what the monthly or quarterly sales quotas are, and an estimate of marketing and other business expenses. In general, I advise people who do direct sales to take a third of their profits and re-invest in their business, one third to put towards their family's financial goals, and save the rest. There are many direct sales companies out there with great products, a good business plan, and excellent sales training. Of course, there are also a few duds out there, so I would recommend researching several companies before making your final decision. DirectSellingNews.com puts out an annual list of the Top 100 Direct Sales Companies, which you can find on their website.

ACTION ITEM

Which of these cash flow boosting ideas are you willing to implement to add fuel to your financial goals?

CHAPTER 18

Are You Eating Your Paycheck?

One of the spending categories which is frequently out of control for my coaching clients is their food budget. If you've been in a grocery store or restaurant lately, I don't need to tell you food prices are on the rise. Sometimes it feels like we're spending so much on groceries and dining out that we're eating our paychecks! This can be especially hard on single parents, retired folks on fixed incomes, and those who are in between jobs. With the average family of four spending about $800 on food every month, we could all use some tips to trim this budget category! Here are four things you can do, when used together, could save you up to 50% on your monthly food bill.

Use Cash. Typically, people spend 15% *more* money when they are shopping with a credit card instead of cash. Because impulse purchases abound at the grocery store, the numbers can be even higher. When you have a fixed amount of cash in your wallet for groceries and dining out, it automatically makes you mindful about what you're buying. This means you will be more likely to compare brands and unit prices at the grocery store, and pass up the $3.00 soda in favor of water the next time you're out to lunch. All of these small choices add up to big time savings over the course of a month. Interestingly, people also tend to purchase healthier food when using cash for groceries. A fatter wallet and slimmer waistline is something we all can be happy about!

Buy Things on Sale, Before You Need Them. Most people buy a particular item at the store when they are out (or almost out) of it at home. It doesn't matter if the item is on sale or not, it has to be purchased this week because we *need* it! Next time you see something your family loves on sale, buy a 90-day supply of it and you'll save a ton of money (just be mindful of product expiration dates.) Here is an example: Your family loves peanut butter! You go through 2 jars of it every month. Your favorite brand is $3.75 per jar which means you spend $22.50 on it every 90 days. Next time the peanut butter goes on sale for $2.00 per jar—don't buy just one: buy six jars! This would only cost you $12.00 for a 3-month supply of peanut butter, a savings of $10.50 ($42.00 for the year). This may not seem like much money saved, but multiply that times all of the items you regularly buy at the grocery store. You can see how this would save you hundreds of dollars, especially if you apply it to your non-food grocery items like deodorant, paper towels, and cleaning products. The one exception to this tip is produce and other perishable food items which cannot be frozen. Be realistic about how much produce your family can reasonably eat before it spoils.

Use Coupons. I can hear your groans from here, "But I don't want to spend hours clipping and organizing coupons, only to forget them at home!" The great news is there's *no scissors required* in today's digital world of coupons. You can access coupons directly from your smart phone with apps from Target, Kroger, Meijer and other retailers. Just show your phone to the cashier; she'll scan the bar code on the screen, and your coupons come right off your order. No more worries about forgetting your coupons at home.

Try Meal Planning. Americans throw away about 30% of the food they buy. That's the equivalent of $150 in food wasted every month—$1,800 for the year! Next time you're scraping food from your plate into the garbage, imagine those are dollars falling into the trash can. By doing some meal planning, you'll drastically reduce the amount of food your family throws away.

Just like managing your time and money, when you manage your food resources on purpose, you'll waste less and save your dollars.

ACTION ITEMS

How much is your family spending on groceries and dining out on a monthly basis? Which of these tips will you start incorporating to help your family save money on your food bill?

CHAPTER 19

Don't Let the Holidays Ruin Your Budget

E motional spending peaks between the Thanksgiving and Christmas holidays. With extra expenses for entertaining, decorating, and gift giving, sometimes the holidays aren't so happy for our budgets. Our best intentions for "behaving" with our money during the holiday season can be thrown off track when family dysfunction rears its ugly head. By being mindful of these financial and emotional landmines well before December, there's a greater likelihood of maneuvering around them so they don't blow up in our faces.

The first and most important thing you can do to prevent a case of "credit card hangover" in the New Year is to put together a holiday budget, preferably by July so you have plenty of time to save. This budget should include gift giving, decorating, and entertaining. If you've never done this, I suggest going online and pulling your credit card and bank statements from November and December of last year to get a starting point. The sooner in the year that you do this, the easier it will be to set aside a small amount of money each pay period so your holiday budget is fully funded by December 1st. Some banks and credit unions still have "Christmas Club" accounts you can utilize for this purpose.

What happens if the holidays are just around the corner, and you realize there's not enough to go around? How do you handle this dilemma? I think it's best to decide as a family, what are the most important things and experiences you want to have this year, and focus your dollars there. Many times we mindlessly spend money on certain things every year out of holiday tradition, but they're really not very meaningful for us. Is it something the whole family *loves* to do?

CASE STUDY: THE NUTCRACKER

Every year, Holly and her family of four go to see a live production of The Nutcracker in December. Last year she noticed her son spent most of the time fidgeting and whining during the show, while her husband snoozed with his head on her shoulder. Was this a good use of their holiday entertainment dollars? Holly and her daughter really love this tradition, so it was decided the two of them would continue to enjoy this tradition together. Holly's husband and son were happy to be let off the hook to stay home and watch football. Everyone's happy and Holly just trimmed some money off of her holiday budget!

The easiest area to save money is holiday decorating. The first Christmas my husband and I were in our current home, we did spend some money on holiday décor. We focused our money on reusable items like silk flowers, an artificial Christmas tree, and a wreath for the door. Our original motivation for purchasing an artificial tree, wreath, and other silk floral items were our cats. We knew Peanut and Little Tiny would be drawn to real plants and try to eat them. However, I now realize how much money this saves us year after year by reusing these great looking decorations. Yes, I usually buy one or two new things every holiday season, but I'm more selective about what I buy because I don't need much. The dollar stores usually have some great seasonal items, like decorative towels, gift wrap and bows, potholders, and kitchenware. I bought a $3 snowman platter for my famous Christmas sugar cookies and I've had it for more than 10 years. No one would know I bought it at The Dollar General unless I told them.

Holiday feasting is one spending category that can definitely escalate quickly. The main rule to keep in mind is to always keep it simple. Don't go overboard on the number of items on the menu. Have friends and family members bring a signature dish so you're not buying all the food. I've found that people love showing off their culinary skills, and most enjoy contributing to the meal. So when someone says, "What can I bring to dinner?" Don't say, "Nothing!" Rather than stocking a full bar of cocktails, wine and beer, make a signature drink or spiked punch bowl instead. If someone doesn't care for what you're serving, they can easily bring a bottle of their favorite wine. If you need extra dishes, glassware, or specialty items such as a turkey platter, see if you can borrow from friends or family instead of buying them.

Gift giving is usually the most emotionally charged area of holiday spending. Write down all of the people for whom you typically purchase gifts. Is there a way for you to whittle down your list?

CASE STUDY: FEWER GIFTS, MORE HAPPY

Several years ago, my stepmom, Francine, suggested a gift exchange instead of buying presents for all of the adults in our family at Christmastime. Now, instead of having to buy six gifts, my husband and I only have to buy two. We also put a price limit on the gifts and pick a theme, like "buy local," or "As Seen on TV." We do the exchange as a white elephant which makes it fun to "steal" the gifts we want from each other.

Don't forget that a gift doesn't have to be expensive to be meaningful. Parents and grandparents especially like personalized and homemade gifts. I've made calendars for parents on both sides of the family with pictures of the kids and grandkids throughout the past year and included everyone's birthdays. Those were always a hit. Be sure to get started early on personalized gifts so you're not stuck paying for expedited shipping to make sure it arrives before Christmas. Homemade baked goods make great presents for coworkers, friends, and teachers.

The holiday season is supposed to be a fun and relaxing time with friends and family. However, overspending on the holidays can cause major stress once the bills come rolling in and all of the fun is over. We can also experience emotions, such as guilt, during this time which can negatively impact our financial health. For example, if you are recently divorced, you may try to make up for not spending as much time with your kids by buying them a pile of presents. Trust me, kids want your time and attention more than your gifts. Take some time to think about what emotional triggers usually cause you to spend more than what you can afford.

Sometimes other people may attempt to put pressure on us to spend more than we'd planned. The best way to handle this is to say, "We're making a concentrated effort to become financially healthy, so we've put some reasonable limits on our holiday spending. This is our budget, and we're going to stick to it." Just by being mindful of these issues before they come up will allow you to choose your response instead of reacting out of emotion. This way you are spending your holiday dollars wisely on the things that are really important to you and your family.

~

Here are some additional tips to ensure the holidays don't ruin your budget. No one wants to wake up in January with a credit card hangover!

- **Make your list and check it twice.** Grab a piece of paper and write down the people for whom you typically purchase a Christmas gift. Now it's time to edit the list. Are you buying for certain people out of guilt or habit? I've noticed as the years pass and family members get married and have kids, more and more people are added to our holiday shopping list. (Somehow, no one ever seems to come off the list!) So if you are still buying for all of your cousins, aunts, uncles, nieces and nephews, it's time to initiate this conversation with your extended family. Thanksgiving is a great time to do this, when everyone's pleasantly full of turkey, stuffing, and pumpkin pie. Chances are they've been thinking the same thing.

- **Make a budget for each person on your list.** Stick to it like glue!
- **Start setting aside money each week for Christmas shopping.** I'm not saying you actually have to start your shopping right now, unless you want to. Transfer the money into a savings account so you don't "accidentally" spend it on something else.
- **Consider shopping at stores with layaway purchase plans for the holidays.** Recently, several large retailers like Wal-Mart have resurrected layaway purchase plans for the holidays. You do your shopping, take your haul to customer service, and they put it in the warehouse for you. You make regular payments on your layaway stash, and only take the merchandise home when it's paid in full. It's like the anti- credit card plan!
- **Shop around.** If you wait until the last minute to do your shopping, you're probably not going to have time to research your purchases and find the best deal. You may be able to snag some Groupons or other deals and coupons to purchase your Christmas gifts at a nice discount. No one but you needs to know that "Santa" scored a 60% off deal!
- **Give the gift of time or effort instead of the usual "stuff."** Most homes in America are already overflowing with more stuff than we need or could possibly use. Of course, kids typically want toys, dolls, and electronics for Christmas, but most adults would appreciate a gift of time or effort instead of more stuff to cram in the closet. If your friend or sister-in-law is a new mom, she'll greatly appreciate a "gift certificate" for several hours of babysitting from you so she can have a much needed night out. Your aging parent would probably enjoy an outing with you to the movies or a museum more than a gift card. We all have gifts and talents other people would appreciate, so be creative!

ACTION ITEMS

What are some strategies you use to keep your holiday gift budget under control? Will you be having a credit card free Christmas this year? What tips discussed in this chapter will your family implement to rein in holiday spending?

CHAPTER 20

Spending Detox

etoxes have become popular in the nutrition circles, and maybe you've done one as I have. Essentially, a dietary detox restricts eating to certain foods and juices for few days or more to reset your metabolism and refresh your body. I always do a food detox right after the holidays because my healthy eating has inevitably gone off track. A brief period of restriction stops out-of-control eating, reverses the damage, and gives me a fresh start. In this same way, a financial detox can be a valuable tool to rein in spending after a binge and reset your motivation.

About once a year, I undertake a "spending detox" —a month-long period of no shopping for anything that's not a true necessity. Many years, I've approached this shopping fast as spending nothing on clothes, shoes, jewelry, cosmetics, books, music, etc. This past year, rather than going cold turkey, I thought I would just restrict myself to a small amount of spending money per week—$20.

Let me explain why I do this spending detox annually. First of all, it helps me to appreciate all of the good things I already have in my possession: plenty of clothes and shoes, books I haven't even cracked open yet, and more than enough lotions and lip glosses, among other things. The second reason I do it is to keep my "inner consumer" in check. We're all bombarded with ads via TV, magazines, the internet, and social media, every single day. Online retailers and brick and mortar stores are making it easier and easier for us to part with our money. Does anyone else have a love/hate relationship with Amazon One-Click besides me? Doing a spending detox makes me stop and think, "Do I really need this?"

Here are my personal rules for my annual spending detox. I can spend $20 per week, for a total of $80 per month on non-necessities. If I happen to receive a rebate check in the mail or earn money on my clothing consignment, I can add it to my spending money. If I have unspent gift cards in my wallet, those purchases do not count towards my $80 total. If I see something I want to buy, but choose not to, I will print a picture of the item from my laptop or tear the page out of the magazine and put it in a folder. At the end of my detox, I'll review those items to see if I *really* still want any of them. I have done this in past years to find that I usually end up only buying about 20% of those "desperately wanted" items after my shopping fast is over.

If you want to attempt to do the spending detox and spend zero money on non-essentials, you may want to try it for a shorter period of time, say one week versus one month. Giving myself a small amount of spending money prevents me from falling off the wagon and scrapping the plan mid-detox.

Here are some things I've learned from my past spending detoxes:

- Carrying cash for splurges is an effective budgeting tool. It makes you think twice about spending and if there's not enough cash, you don't buy it.
- Digital shopping is a big temptation for me! I definitely need to set firm monthly limits for those purchases. I am inundated with daily emails from my favorite stores announcing the *final day* of the big sale! (Buy now, now, now!) I have unsubscribed from some email lists and limited others to once a week or once a month emails. The less temptation, the better!
- I don't end up buying many of the things I thought I so desperately wanted after my spending detox is over.

- I also tend to be very pleased with the things I do decide to purchase after the spending detox is over.

The purpose of the financial detox is to return us to a mindful state of spending after a period of unrestraint. It can help reset our motivation and balance our saving and spending habits. Just as with a food detox, I don't recommend extending a spending detox beyond 30 days. If you deprive yourself for too long, the detox, whether nutritional or financial, can end up doing more harm than good.

ACTION ITEMS

Do you think a spending detox would be beneficial for you? If so, decide when you will do it, how much discretionary spending money you'll have (if any) per week, and how many days your spending detox will last.

CHAPTER 21

What to Do with a Windfall

We fantasize about being the recipient of a large financial windfall: winning the lottery, getting a huge bonus at work, receiving an inheritance from a long lost relative. We dream about what we'd spend all the money on: luxury cars, oceanfront property, trips to exotic places. In truth, a financial windfall can actually be a source of stress if we are not operating from a detailed Financial Roadmap.

Certainly, we may receive an unexpected cash infusion from a positive source, such as a bonus, gift, or unanticipated tax break. However, not all windfalls are from such positive events. Your windfall could be collecting on an insurance policy or an inheritance due to the death of your spouse, sibling, or parent. Perhaps your cash infusion is due to a divorce or other legal settlement. It's during these emotional times that our risk of making a bad financial decision skyrockets.

"The problems that can arise as a result of sudden wealth rarely are the result of the money; they are almost always psychological, emotional, and relational," says Robert Pagliarini in his book *The Sudden Wealth Solution: 12 Principles to Transform Sudden Wealth into Lasting Wealth*. Whether your windfall is from a positive or negative source, there are common steps to take to safeguard yourself from these emotional money landmines.

- Ensure your Financial Roadmap is in place. It's a mistake to not have a budget set up and your debt reduction and savings goals spelled out. If you don't have a plan, you may end up wasting money from a windfall.
- Consult someone who can objectively look at your *entire* money situation such as a financial coach, CPA, or financial planner (maybe even all three) before making any major decisions. There may be unforeseen tax consequences or liabilities related to your windfall of which you need to be aware. Well-meaning friends and family will likely offer their opinions and advice; however, it's wise to consult an expert who has a handle on all of the moving parts of your financial picture.
- Use the Overflow List concept from "The Income Rollercoaster" chapter to help you set priorities of what to do with the windfall. Make sure these things are in support of your goals to eliminate your consumer debt and build up your savings.
- I strongly recommend against making any major money decisions, if at all possible, within the first six months of a traumatic event which leads to a windfall. Your first priority is to take care of yourself and your family. When I have a client who is dealing with the death of a spouse or other loved one, I highly recommend they seek out counseling or a grief support group. There are times when postponing a money decision can indeed be the best decision.

CASE STUDY: THE SUDDEN WIDOW

"Joan," age 51, unexpectedly lost her seemingly healthy husband to a heart attack. She came to me for financial coaching because she was about to receive the payout from two different life insurance policies, and she was unsure about what to do with the money. Joan and her husband did have a few credit cards with balances and a mortgage. They also owned several acres of land on which they had planned to build their dream home.

Joan was very emotional regarding the piece of land she owned. She wanted to put it up for sale because "our dream house isn't going to happen now that my husband is gone." I cautioned her against selling this piece of land because the cost of property taxes and maintenance was very low. I could see she was in danger of making an emotional decision about it, and there was really no pressing need to sell it. The insurance proceeds easily paid off her non-mortgage debt and gave her more than a year's worth of income in savings. Joan wasn't sure if she wanted to continue to live in her current house, although she could certainly afford to stay there. I advised her *not* to make any decision regarding the sale of her current home for at least six months. We only tackled the financial details that truly had to be handled right away, such as transferring her husband's 401(k) to an IRA for Joan and finding her a good investment advisor to help her manage it.

Fast forward 18 months… Joan received a fantastic job offer 50 miles away and accepted it. She is currently renting a condo in this new town, while looking for a permanent home. Joan used some of the remaining money from the insurance proceeds to pay off her home, which she is renting to her son and daughter-in-law. Her former residence is now a source of passive cash flow for Joan. Her son has also purchased the land from her and is planning on building *his* dream home there. The plot of land Joan's husband dearly loved will be staying in the family after all, providing a home for their children and grandchildren.

No matter the source of a windfall, be sure to consult with a trusted money advisor and postpone big decisions that could be made in the heat of emotion. If the windfall is due to a negative event, such as the death of a loved one, I strongly encourage you to seek the guidance of a counselor or therapist.

ACTION ITEMS

It's best to take your time to find a trustworthy money coach, CPA, and/ or financial planner *before* you need them. If you don't have these people on your team, ask friends and family members for recommendations. If you know you will be receiving a large influx of cash soon, I highly recommend reading *The Sudden Wealth Solution: 12 Principles to Transform Sudden Wealth into Lasting Wealth* by Robert Pagliarini.

CHAPTER 22

Is It Possible to Enjoy Paying Your Bills?

"*Enjoy paying my bills? No way!*" I used to think the same thing. Several years ago, I did a book study of *The Magic* by Rhonda Byrne (author of *The Secret*) with a group of friends online. The subject matter: developing a positive money consciousness and creating an attitude of abundance and gratitude. One of the exercises in the book study had a lasting impact on my attitude toward paying my bills. In a nutshell, when you are paying your bills, you do two things.

1. Write in the memo line of the check—or if there is a memo line for online bill pay—"Thank You." Why? You are thanking the company and its employees for providing you a service: electricity, insurance protection, clean water, a roof over your head. Doing this reminds you to be grateful for the services you're receiving and that your use of the service employs people and enables them to provide for their families.

2. Before filing it away, write on the bill itself, "Thank you for the money." In doing this, you are thanking God for blessing you with the money to pay your bills. It is a

reminder to be grateful for the financial resources you already have at your disposal.

By doing these two things, it has created in me a greater sense of gratitude for my financial blessings. Here are some additional ways to make bill paying less of a chore and a little more enjoyable:

- Pay your bills in a pleasant environment. I usually do this in my home office, which is filled with many of my favorite things. I have a nice steaming cup of coffee at my side and play music I enjoy while I'm paying the bills.
- Chose a day and time when you are alert and calm. I typically do this on Saturday mornings. If you are feeling rushed, stressed out, or tired you will associate those feelings with the act of bill paying and dread it even more the next time it rolls around.
- Use a good pen to write out your bills and balance your checkbook. There's nothing like a fancy pen to make you feel important. Whether you use a cute pen with purple ink or a pen fit for a Fortune 500 CEO, using a pen you love to conduct your personal financial transactions makes bill paying seem less like drudgery.
- Splurge on some personalized checks. When my husband and I switched banks over a year ago, we received free standard checks. I was actually overjoyed when I finally ran out of those boring, plain checks! There are endless designs you can choose, from Mickey Mouse to Harley Davidson. You can even upload your own photos to create checks with pictures of your kids, pets, or favorite vacation photos. Why not use some of your vision board pictures for your checks as a reminder of your goals? Pick a design that will make you smile every time you need to a write check to pay a bill.

Will there ever come a day when you are truly excited to pay your bills? Maybe not. However, you need to pay your bills anyway, so why not make it as pleasant as possible?

ACTION ITEM

Which of the tips mentioned in this chapter will you apply the next time you pay your bills?

CHAPTER 23

Troubleshooting Your Budget

What do you do when your spending plan doesn't seem to be working and you're frustrated and ready to throw in the towel? The first thing you need to remember is *no one does this perfectly*. Budgeting is an art, not an exact science. Life happens and sometimes it means midcourse corrections will have to be made on your financial journey. The longer you budget, the easier it will be for you.

I want to make you aware of seven potential budget pitfalls you may encounter on your journey to your Preferred Financial Destination and how to avoid them. I'll also give you the corresponding lifelines, which will pull you out of those pits and get you back on the road to success.

Pitfall #1–You're unaware of what you're spending as you go through the month, which causes you to go over budget on entertainment, dining out, clothing, or another category. We have a vague feeling we *might* be spending too much money in a certain area, but we're just not sure. This can be especially true if both husband and wife are spending money in the same category and are unaware of what the other one is spending. So what is the solution?

Lifeline #1–Use cash or prepaid credit cards for the categories you have a tendency to overspend on. Typically, we're not tempted to overspend on things like rent or gas for the car. It's usually the food, clothing, and entertainment categories that are hard to tame. The easiest way to do this is to use cash for these things. Paying with cash at the register hurts—and that's a good thing! Why? Because it causes us to be *mindful* about our spending. If you are nervous about carrying around cash, I completely understand. Prepaid credit cards or a separate account with a debit card may be a better option for you. You can transfer a set amount every time you get paid for your entertainment, dining out, clothing, etc. This way you can't spend more than your budget, because when it's gone, it's gone! When you set up your first budget, decide ahead of time which categories will be paid with cash (or prepaid credit card), via check, online bill pay, or direct withdraw.

Pitfall #2–You forget something that should be in your spending plan. Graduation pictures, your parents' anniversary, a cousin's baby shower… Expenses like this tend to sneak up on us and throw our budgets out of whack.

Lifeline #2–Tweak your budget to see what other categories you can adjust down to make up for the shortfall. Your budget is not static! Be creative and consider all the possibilities to cover the unexpected expense. When these unplanned expenditures come up, ask yourself these questions:

- Do I really need to spend money on this?
- What's the least amount I can spend?
- Can I work some overtime to help pay for this?

We can feel pressured by others to spend money in social or family situations. You must be determined to take ownership over your financial journey. This may mean saying no to a few things, so you can say yes to the things that are important to you.

Pitfall #3–You budget for perfect conditions and not reality.

Lifeline #3–Be realistic about your goals and lifestyle. If you allocate $0 for Dining Out that's probably not realistic. Don't cut out fun completely; just put some reasonable limits on it. If you set up your spending plan with nothing in the entertainment, dining out, or other fun categories, you're setting yourself up for burnout. If you go on a diet, and you can never have a piece of cake, how long will you last before you fall off the wagon? Maybe a few days? It's okay to have portion controlled fun built into your budget in the same way it's okay to have a piece of cake every once in a while (just not every day, with every meal!) Understand that your budget will change from month to month. June is nothing like December when it comes to how you're spending your money! You need to adjust your budget month to month to reflect it.

Pitfall #4–You create your monthly budget, and then ignore it.

Lifeline #4–Hold weekly reviews with your spouse or partner for the first few months. If you are single, find someone who will be your accountability partner. Schedule a set time to have them call you and ask how things are going with your spending plan. Cementing a new habit takes effort the first few months. Be sure to choose a budgeting tool that makes it easy for you to stay on top of things. Technology is your friend! I use my bank's online budget tool, so I can easily access monthly spending from my laptop, tablet or phone. My bank even texts me if I am in danger of going over my limit for a certain category. If you've selected a budget tool you're struggling to use, switch to a different format. The right tool will make it *less stressful* for you to budget.

Pitfall #5–You experience wild swings in certain bills, such as utilities.

Lifeline #5–Sign up for even billing. When we have uncertainty revolving around a particular monthly bill, it can cause major stress! I typically see this with utility bills in older, less energy-efficient homes. People cringe when they see this bill in the mailbox because they never know what to expect! The easy way to resolve this is to sign up for even billing.

Pitfall #6–You have the majority of your bills due all at the same time.

Lifeline #6–Request due date changes. Is your cash very tight for the first pay period of the month? For my coaching clients who get paid twice a month, it's common for me to see that one pay period is really tight on cash after the bills are paid and the other pay period is flush with spending money. These folks have enough money every month to pay all the bills and then some, but the cash flow isn't balanced from pay period to pay period. The easy solution is to call and see about getting due dates changed on credit card accounts or utility bills to smooth out cash flow. Shifting due dates on one or two bills might make all the difference in the world and you'll feel less stressed! Most companies are happy to bump your due date out 10 to 15 days.

Pitfall #7–You live paycheck-to-paycheck but receive several thousand dollars for your tax refund.

Lifeline #7–Talk to your CPA or tax professional about adjusting your withholdings on your paycheck so your refund is as small as possible (without owing the IRS). If you normally get a $5,000 refund, that's over $400 of monthly cash flow! Why struggle to make ends meet 11 months out of the year and allow the government to hang onto your money interest-free? Use the extra money every month to pay off debt and pad your emergency fund instead.

ACTION ITEMS

Ask yourself the following questions: Which of the seven pitfalls am I experiencing right now? Which have I struggled with in the past? Which lifelines do I need to employ to help me stay on track to financial health?

PART THREE

Living Debt Free

CHAPTER 24

The Brief History of Debt

In today's society, it seems like credit cards, car payments, and home equity loans are woven into the fabric of our daily lives. In fact, we may look at someone with a mixture of shock and awe if they say they don't have any credit cards or they paid cash for a new car. I haven't had any credit cards in over a decade. When this fact comes up in conversation, I get weird looks and questions like, "Do you shop online? How can you travel without a credit card?" It's interesting as a society, we have been conditioned to believe that having and using debt is a normal way of life. But it didn't always used to be this way.

Did you know the mortgage industry came into being in the 1930's? Did you know the first credit card was "born" in 1950? Did you know borrowing money was deeply frowned upon and even considered *scandalous* less than a hundred years ago? I was a little stunned the first time I learned these facts. In the spectrum of the history of money, debt as we know it is a very recent and small blip on the radar. People have been using some form of money for almost 5,000 years, yet credit cards and mortgages are less than 100 years old! How did people survive back in the "good old days?" The answer is simple: they saved up and paid cash for the things they wanted.

HISTORY OF MONEY TIMELINE:

2500 BC–Gold & silver rings used for trade
650 BC–First minted coins
1600s–First paper money and national bank
1934–Modern mortgages became widely available
1950–First credit card: Diners Club
1970–Only 15% of Americans had a credit card
Now–Debt is a way of life. You can finance anything and everything!

As you can see from this timeline, debt products are relative newcomers to the world's economy. And yet, many of us consider our credit cards, car loans, and mortgages to be an indispensable part of our financial lives. Why? We've been conditioned through advertising that financing our purchases is a way of life. Here's the truth: debt is a product sold by banks and other lending institutions.

The following quote appeared in a 1910 Sears catalog: *"Buying on credit is folly."* Today, many retailers make more profit on financing than on the actual sale of their products. What a change in just over a hundred years! Try this little experiment next time you are watching TV: count every commercial selling debt in some shape or form. Listen for cues like "No down payment! Easy monthly payments! No interest for 36 months!" I recently did this and counted 16 commercials selling debt (credit cards, car financing, furniture with easy monthly payments) during a one hour TV program. That's one debt commercial every 3 minutes and 45 seconds! Companies use debt as leverage to sell their products. It is very easy to mindlessly go into debt for things we really don't need or even want. How many times have you regretted buying something you charged on a credit card?

CASE STUDY: "EASY" MONEY

I fell into this trap myself as a young adult. I thought I hit the jackpot when I was approved for my first Citibank credit card as a college freshman. It didn't take long for other credit card offers to come my way: Dillard's, Victoria's Secret, American Express. A few years later, I consolidated them into one loan. The only problem is I didn't close the cards when I paid them off. When I hit financial rock bottom four years after I graduated, the credit cards were all maxed out again, plus I was still paying on the consolidation loan. The sad thing is I really had nothing of value to show for those debts. I was mindlessly spending on things I really didn't need, because that's what I thought being an adult was all about.

If you want to reduce or eliminate your debt, your first step is becoming *mindful* about debt and how it is being marketed to you on a daily basis.

ACTION ITEMS

Think about your attitudes and emotions regarding debt. Have you always thought debt was a normal part of everyone's financial life? Are you surprised living debt free was the norm a hundred years ago? Try counting the number of debt-related commercials during an hour of TV-watching.

CHAPTER 25

Debt is Dangerous to Your Financial Health

E xcessive debt can have the same effect on your financial health as a physical disease has on your body. In fact, I frequently say debt is like a *financial cancer*. Once you start borrowing, debt seems to multiply on its own. If you don't take swift action, your debt can grow out of control and begin gnawing away at your financial health. Some people choose to bury their heads in the sand, trying to ignore the situation. When their financial health flatlines and the only option is bankruptcy, they wonder what happened.

We have the common sense to know that cancer inside of our bodies will *not* go away if we ignore it and do nothing. A good doctor will lay out an aggressive treatment plan which must start immediately, when his patient is diagnosed. There's no time to waste—the situation is serious and it's battle time! We need to have a similar attitude when it comes to attacking our debt.

Here's another way to look at it. When we are saddled with a large amount of debt, it's like carrying around an extra 50 or 100 pounds. Though not life-threatening, this burden puts extra stress on your physical, mental, and emotional health. We may not even realize the weight we are carrying. Imagine if you were going about your daily tasks with a 50-pound weight strapped to your back. It would make even simple tasks more laborious—walking, bending over, carrying groceries into the house. Some people have been carrying around the extra weight of debt with them for so long, they can't even imagine how light and free they would feel if it were suddenly gone.

Just as carrying around excess body weight has a myriad of negative effects, debt can be hazardous to *both* our physical and our financial health. More than 50% of us see our money situation as a significant source of chronic stress. People who experience high stress regarding their debt are twice as likely to suffer a heart attack as were those people who don't worry about their finances. Those folks with chronic money stress also experience an increased likelihood of ulcers, migraines, depression, insomnia, and lower back pain.

When I was trying to outrun my avalanche of debt, stress and insomnia were my constant companions. It wasn't until I was on the path to financial wellness for over a year that I realized how much stress my debt had been causing me on a daily basis. I used to worry about money constantly, and it was taking a toll on me physically, mentally, and emotionally.

Why is debt so dangerous to our financial health? *It's because debt gnaws away at our income like a cancer, making it difficult to save and invest for the future.* Many people are not saving enough for retirement or other long term goals because their income is consumed by car payments, credit card bills, and home equity line payments. If your entire paycheck is eaten up by debt payments, it's hard to get ahead. When you are debt free, even someone with a modest income can do some serious wealth building and enjoy a comfortable retirement.

Thomas J. Stanley, Ph. D., author of *The Millionaire Mind*, surveyed the country's top millionaires and asked them what was the one key to building wealth. A whopping 78% of them said it was *getting and staying debt free*! Why do you think these millionaires would say being debt free is the key to their success? I believe it's because they *truly* understand the cost of debt. When most of us think about the price of monthly payments, we are *only* considering the interest rate. The average credit card rate is currently 15%, and that doesn't seem too bad—right? But it's not the only cost of debt. When we make purchases on credit, we typically spend 15% more than we would with cash! Paying with cash hurts, literally. Scientists have discovered when people make purchases with cash, it actually registers as pain in our brains. This tends to make us mindful of our purchases. This is not the case when buying on credit, so we tend to spend more.

Too much debt prevents us from saving for the future: for emergencies, investments, college, and retirement. The other cost of debt most of us don't consider is *opportunity cost*. When we are paying credit card interest and overspending on things we really don't need, we are losing out on the opportunity to save and invest. Financial advisors generally agree a 10% return is reasonable to expect from your long term investments. This means the true cost of debt can be as much as 40%: the interest rate (15%) + overspending (15%) + missed opportunity (10%). And, if we fail to save for emergencies and college expenses, we end up going into debt to pay for them. This can become a dangerous and vicious cycle.

Once we break this cycle of mindless debt accumulation, we start down the road to financial health. As we pay off our credit cards and other debts, more of our income is freed up to save and invest for a brighter future. Take a moment to reflect on your physical health, your stress level, and your debt. Are you currently suffering from any of the health concerns I mentioned earlier? Here is the good news: when you shed the weight of excess debt, you'll stress less, sleep better, and feel great!

ACTION ITEMS

Ask yourself the following questions: How often do I worry about my money situation? Do I lose sleep over financial issues? Is money stress affecting my health? If I woke up debt free tomorrow, how would that make me feel? Add up your household's current monthly payments for non-mortgage debt. If you were debt-free, what would you do with the extra money each month?

CHAPTER 26

What's in Your Wallet: Credit, Debit, or Cash?

W hat's in your wallet? Credit, debit, cash, or all three? You might think only cavemen and conspiracy theorists would live their financial lives off the grid and not have a credit card. Certainly credit cards make it simple for us to pay for things, but they also make it very convenient for us to spend more than we intend to and go into debt as a result.

Credit cards are unsecured, meaning there is no particular asset standing behind the debt as collateral, unlike a mortgage or car loan. This type of debt is riskier for the bank, because it's harder for them to collect if you don't make the agreed monthly payments. This means higher interest rates for you!

The most common type of unsecured debt is the bank issued credit card. These credit cards—Visa®, MasterCard®, American Express®, and Discover®—can be used almost anywhere and you can purchase pretty much anything and everything you need or want. It's so easy to mindlessly charge away with our bank credit cards as we go about our daily lives.

Retailers attempt to lure us into signing up for their store charge cards by dangling coupons, discounts, and special offers in front of us. We may think we are taking advantage of these stores by cashing in on these sweet deals, but these credit cards clock in an average interest rate of over 24%! Even if you pay off your balance in full every month, retailers know coupons and special offers will bring you into their stores and onto their websites more often. Credit cards are the equivalent of playing with financial fire. Only 29% of us are paying off our credit card balances every month, according to the American Bankers Association.

So, if you choose to have a credit card, carefully monitor your spending and pay the balance off in full monthly.

Credit is ever evolving and we're starting to see payment methods that don't even require a physical card to be present, just your mobile phone. Not too far into the future we will be paying for groceries with our thumbprints, which will be linked to a credit account with a bank somewhere else in the country. Convenience is normally a great thing, but these methods of payment are making it even easier to mindlessly spend. They are further disconnecting us from our money. The less a transaction "seems" like spending money, the more likely we are to overspend.

~

The debit card has a tendency to be viewed as the redheaded stepchild of the financial world. I believe this is because of two big myths associated with debit cards, and both have to do with the safety of your money.

The first myth is that it is unsafe to use your debit card online. Many personal finance gurus perpetuate this myth to their followers. It is true that credit cards offer extra layers of protection, but it doesn't mean it's unsafe to use a debit card. You can make your online debit purchases safer by following these tips:

- Shop only on secure websites, which will start with "https." If the "s" is not there in the URL, the site is not encrypted and vulnerable to cyber thieves.
- *Don't* save your debit card number on merchant sites. Yes, it makes it convenient for future use, but it also puts

you at risk if the retailer's payment information gets hacked.

- Keep a close eye on your account transactions and report any suspicious activity *immediately*.
- Consider using PayPal for online purchases, which links directly to your bank account like a debit card, without exposing your account numbers.

The second debit card myth is that your money is unrecoverable if thieves use your information fraudulently. If you report a fraudulent charge within two business days to your financial institution, your liability is capped at $50. This is why you should keep a close eye on your bank account. If you wait more than two business days, but no longer than 60 days, your liability is capped at $500. Check with your bank, as they may offer additional protection over and above these general limits. Here are some ways to limit your fraud liability with debit card transactions:

- When swiping your card at a store, always choose to process it as a "credit." By doing so, you're covered by Visa or MasterCard's zero-liability policy and will have no responsibility for unauthorized transactions. You do not get this same protection if you select "debit" and enter your PIN.
- Consider keeping less money in the checking account that is connected to the debit card. My husband and I have the majority of our funds in a savings account and keep a relatively small cash cushion in the accounts that have debit cards attached to them. This severely limits the amount of damage a cyber thief could do if he accessed our debit card information.
- Memorize your PIN and do not carry it with you. If you lose your wallet and it has both your debit card and PIN in it, you've just given a criminal the equivalent of a free pass to Disney World!

The debit card has some unique advantages. It's safer than carrying cash or even checks, and is certainly more convenient. The best advantage to using a debit card over a credit card is *it won't allow you to go into debt!*

~

Is cash really king? Well, consider this: when you make purchases with cash, it actually registers as pain in your brain. That's actually a good thing, and we can use it in our favor to control our spending. When people use credit cards instead of cash, they typically spend more. You're probably sick and tired of hearing it, but I want you to remember the cost of credit purchases. Cash can be a great way to impose some discipline on yourself, because you'll think twice before parting with those Benjamins!

Nervous about carrying around a lot of cash? No worries! You don't need to give up your checks or debit cards. I recommend using cash only for those budget categories which have a tendency to get out of control: food, entertainment, clothing, etc. Another option is to transfer your spending money to a prepaid credit card or a separate account with a debit card. This way you won't "accidentally" spend money that was earmarked for another purpose. Try using cash for one or two categories and see if you don't start saving money immediately!

ACTION ITEM

It's time to become reacquainted with your cash. Try this experiment for the next week. Figure out what spending money you'll need. Go to the ATM, and take it out as cash. Be mindful of respecting the bills, folding them neatly in your wallet, and note your thoughts and feelings as you spend it throughout the week.

CHAPTER 27

Driving a Car without a Payment

Why do so many of us make unwise financial decisions when it comes to buying cars? Owning a car or truck is part of the American way of life, and we can be very attached to our vehicles. It's a rite of passage to get your driver's license and your first car. We may even name our cars and spend countless hours under the hood installing aftermarket upgrades or detailing the interior. We attend car shows and subscribe to auto magazines. Many of us are fiercely loyal to certain brands and models. We see our vehicles as an expression of our personality and an extension of our personal brand.

We even unconsciously judge people by their cars. When I say, "soccer mom," you're probably going to picture her driving a minivan or SUV with plenty of kid-friendly features. You'll probably assume a cattle rancher owns a big Ford or Chevy truck, and a Wall Street stockbroker owns a Mercedes or a Porsche. There's nothing wrong with choosing a vehicle to fit your current lifestyle and preferences. I certainly don't want you to drive an ugly car you hate. However, I do want you to drive a car you can reasonably afford, and I'd love for you to pay cash for it!

What we fail to remember is that a car is *transportation*, first and foremost. There are many options for getting from Point A to Point B, and our primary goal when selecting a vehicle is answering the question, "Can I afford it?" Unfortunately, when many of us say, "Yes, I can afford it," we mean, "I can afford the payments." But what happens if we lose our job or have a cut in income? Then suddenly, we can't afford it and we go into crisis mode.

~

According to Edmunds.com, the average monthly payment on a new vehicle is $479. If you have two vehicles with loans in your household, your car payments could easily meet or exceed your rent or mortgage payment! That's a lot of cash going out each and every month; it would be better spent paying down debt or building up savings.

Most of us have been conditioned to believe that having a car payment is a way of life. This was my mindset before I hit financial rock bottom. When the end of my car payment booklet came, I couldn't wait to get to the dealer to shop for something newer and get right back on the monthly payment bandwagon.

A more serious problem occurs when the value of your vehicle decreases faster than the amount of your loan. According to Kelly Blue Book, as many as half of new car buyers walk into the showroom upside down on their current vehicles, meaning they owe more on their vehicles than they are worth. Unfortunately, this situation is compounded by a dealer's willingness to do "rollover loans" in order to sell you a new car. This means if you are $2,000 upside down on your trade-in, the dealer will roll over the amount and tack it on to your new loan. If you do this two or three times over a several year period, it's easy to see how someone could find themselves owing thousands of dollars more than what their car is worth. Avoid this by choosing the shortest financing term to fit your budget, not the longest! If you are in an upside down car situation right now, you're going to have to hang tight and pay extra on the principal in order to rectify the situation.

~

DID YOU KNOW…?

- Car loans account for the majority of the non-mortgage secured debt in America.
- If you invested the average car payment—$479 per month—at 8% from age 18 to age 78, you would have $7,779,747.56. That's right—almost $8 million! Check it out for yourself here: https://www.daveramsey.com/blog/investing-calculator/
- As many as 50% of new car buyers walk into the showroom upside down on their current vehicles. Kelly Blue Book offers some valuable advice and options for getting out of the "upside down car" here: http://www.kbb.com/car-advice/articles/upside_down-on-a-loan/
- Most car dealers don't make the bulk of their profits on the sale of a new car. The big profit usually comes through financing, selling add-ons, and making money on your trade-in, according to RealCarTips.com.
- Leasing is the worst and most expensive way to "buy" a car. You make payments on something you never own. Leases allow you to drive a car you can't afford to buy. Dealers make their best profits on leased vehicles.
- Don't fall for the 0% interest gimmick! Car dealers make it up in the selling price of the vehicle. Do not be deceived! They are in this business to make a profit!

~

Is it possible to buy a car without a car payment? Yes, it is! I know from personal experience because the vehicles my husband and I own were paid for with cash up front. They are safe, reliable, and nice looking cars. Paying cash for a car doesn't mean it's a junky rust-bucket.

The method of buying a car without a payment requires patience and discipline. However, I can tell you that once you have purchased a car with cash, you'll *never* want to go back to car payments. The process, though not easy, is simple. When your current vehicle is paid off, take the car payment you used to send to the bank and put it in a savings account instead. If your payment is the average of $479, you will have over $5,700 in your account at the end of 12 months. Even if you have some major repairs to the car, you'll still have several thousand dollars in your vehicle savings fund. If your car is in relatively decent condition, you can keep driving it as you pile up cash in your savings account to buy your next vehicle without a car payment!

Yes, this method of buying a car requires both patience and discipline. This can be difficult because many of us are emotionally attached to our cars. We must remember a car is transportation, first and foremost. Don't let "driving in style" drive you straight into the poorhouse!

I urge you to seriously consider keeping your current car for several years after you have paid it off and save the car payments you would have made towards your next debt-free car! In fact, I want you to put a picture of your dream car you'll purchase with cash on your Financial Vision Board.

ACTION ITEMS

What is my monthly car payment? How much do I owe on my car? How much is it currently worth? Why did I choose to buy this particular vehicle—because I could afford it or because it was "my style?" How would it feel to be driving a car without a payment?

CHAPTER 28

Student Loans: Debt with a Purpose?

The current average student loan debt of graduating college seniors is $33,000 and steadily climbing. That's a huge debt to be carrying into your young adult life. It really hurts my heart to see young couples in their late 20s and early 30s who cannot afford to buy a house because they are being crushed under a mountain of student loan debt. And many times, one or both of them are not even working in the field in which they received their degree.

I've also seen parents in their 40s and 50s blow through retirement funds and wrack up mountains of debt in order to put their kids through college. This is even worse than the first scenario, because parents have fewer working years ahead of them to rectify the situation. They run the risk of running out of money in their elder years, which means those kids they put through college are going to have to take care of them financially. (And eldercare expenses can make college costs look like small potatoes!)

My goal is to give both students and parents some direction and tips for ensuring the education they are paying for (not overpaying for) is going to be a source of positive income. This is why I refer to student loans as "debt with a purpose." As with any debt, my advice remains the same: *borrow the least amount of money you need and pay it back as quickly as possible!*

~

What you don't know about the college testing, application, and admissions process *will* hurt you financially. Many parents and students assume they know how the system works... And we all know what happens when you assume! Different colleges have different admissions processes and academic benchmarks—and they can change them at any time. Even if you already have one child at a university now, things may change by the time your high school sophomore is college bound. Consulting an expert and attending classes or seminars on these timely topics is vital for parents of high schoolers.

Waiting too long to act will also hurt you financially. You need to calculate your family's Expected Family Contribution (also known as your EFC) as soon as possible. Parents' idea of what they can afford and the government's calculation of what your family can "afford" might be worlds apart. And, trust me; it's not going to be a pleasant surprise! You need ample time to prepare, save, and make decisions. Plus, waiting too long to act may cause you to miss deadlines for testing and applications, which could lock your child out of their school of choice.

It's a wise idea to have your teenager take an occupational assessment. These tests help to determine what types of careers are a good fit for your child's natural skills and personality. I did this in high school and it was spot-on about my affinity for numbers and I ended up graduating college with an Accounting degree.

Find out *exactly* what type of education, training, and experience is preferred by employers in your child's desired profession. Don't assume you know this just because the high school guidance counselor told you so. Talk to people who are already working and successful in this career path. Contact the hiring manager at companies in the industry and ask them what type of education and experience they're looking for on resumes.

There are many well-paying professions that do not require a four-year degree!

CASE STUDY: THE HANDS-ON LEARNER

My brother Jim, a stellar soccer player, was always an average student in high school. After graduation, he enrolled in a four-year local college for a semester, but was really struggling to keep up with schoolwork. My brother has always been a hands-on learner and has spectacular people skills. Sitting in a desk all day, studying for tests and taking notes for another four years seemed like torture to him. Fortunately, my parents were wise enough to encourage him to consider an alternative: a two-year technical degree in Industrial Electronics. Jim enjoyed the hands-on classroom environment and went to work wiring complex machines for the aerospace industry when he graduated. His excellent people skills did not go unnoticed, and he eventually moved into the Sales Department. My brother is now the Vice President of Sales and Marketing for a machine tool company, making more in salary than many of his friends who have four-year degrees.

This is why it's important to evaluate your child's skills, abilities, and interests to ensure he or she is heading down the right career path and going to receive the type of education and training employers desire. The biggest tragedy is racking up a ton of student loan debt for a degree and then not being able to find work in your field. I've seen it happen and it's very disheartening when you send in those payments month after month for an education you're not even using.

Parents, no matter the age of your children, start loading money into tax favored educational accounts now. Talk with your investment advisor and CPA; they will help you determine which accounts are best for your situation and what types of investments to hold within the accounts. Save early and save often! This will drastically reduce or eliminate the need for your kids to incur student loan debt for their education.

~

What if I'm heading off to college soon and there's little or no money saved up? My advice, although not very popular, is very effective for paying for an education: *Get a job!* I'm not sure where the myth originated, but it's become popular opinion that students should focus solely on their studies because working is going to negatively impact their grades. Research has shown the *opposite* is actually true! College students who work part time (20 hours or less) actually have better grades than those who don't work at all. Plus, they are learning job skills, time management, life skills, and earning money to put towards their education. Sounds like an all-around win to me! Personally, I always had a job when I was in college. My husband worked two part-time jobs to put himself through technical school without student loan debt or help from his parents. Was it hard? Yes. Can it be done? Absolutely!

Even better, find a part-time job related to your field of study. If you're in nursing school, get a part-time job in a local hospital, even if it's working in the cafeteria. You'll make valuable connections which could help your career later on. See if you can find a job with tuition reimbursement. I worked in collections at a national bank while in college. Trust me, it wasn't exactly a fun job, but I had 80% tuition reimbursement. That job is part of the reason why I graduated from college without student loans! Research employment opportunities at the university you want to attend. You'll earn extra money on campus, plus you may even get reduced tuition.

In-state universities are always a better deal than out-of-state schools, unless you have a scholarship. Crossing a state line to go to school could easily double your student loan payments! Don't assume a more "prestigious" (expensive) school is going to give you an edge in the job market. As a former HR Manager, I can tell you the majority of employers are more concerned with the fact that you have a degree than the particular school you attended.

Consider taking your basic requirement classes at an affiliated community college. The cost per credit hour is typically one-half to one-third of the cost of most universities.

Just be absolutely sure the credits will transfer to your university of choice! By attending a community college for the first year or two of your education, you can save yourself a bundle, plus your diploma will only have the name of the university from which you graduated.

Once you have decided on a school, weigh on-campus versus off-campus living costs. If you're going to a local school, living at home can save both kids and parents a small fortune! This useful calculator will help you crunch the numbers to compare costs: http://www.calcxml.com/calculators/living-on-or-off-campus?skn=124

If your kids are just entering high school, tutoring may be a worthwhile investment. Getting good grades in high school matters when it comes to scoring scholarships! It's rare for someone to get a full ride scholarship these days. However, there are all kinds of partial scholarship opportunities for sports, heritage, alumni, civic club membership, and academic achievement. It does take some research to track them down and effort to apply, but the payoff means less student loan debt. It also pays to take classes which help students prepare for ACT, SAT, and other entrance tests. Better scores mean more scholarship opportunities.

~

Decisions about college can be fraught with emotion. As parents, we may want our children to graduate from our alma mater or join the same fraternity or sorority as we did. We may want only the best for our kids, no matter the cost. Your daughter may want to attend a particular university because many of her friends are going there. *It's time to stop and take a deep breath.* I know this may sound heretical, but there is no law stating you have to pay for your child's college education. Of course, if you can contribute and help your kids avoid student loan debt that is certainly a great thing. Making an emotional decision about college will end up costing you both in dollars and stress. There are objective college experts who can assist your family with analyzing the pros and cons, and help you arrive at a wise decision. A good college expert can easily save your family five to ten times their consulting fee.

Dan Bisig, co-author of *College Entrance Game Plan: Your Comprehensive Guide to Collecting, Organizing and Funding College*, says it best: "Parents, do not allow your teenager to make a $40,000 to $280,000 decision for your family!" Think back to how impulsive and emotional you were as a 16 to 18-year-old. Were you in any position to make such a financially momentous decision? I sure wasn't. I remember being 17 years old, my parents freshly divorced, and having the college talk. I really wanted to go to Miami University in Oxford, Ohio, and live on campus. I fell in love with the campus when I went there for a high school retreat. Unfortunately, Miami University was four times the price of Northern Kentucky University (NKU,) and I had a 2-year scholarship to the latter. Yes, I graduated with honors from NKU and it was a great educational experience. However, at 17, I cried and told my parents it was "no fair" and they were "mean" for "ruining my dreams" of an idyllic university experience. I am firmly convinced my parents made the right call *by not letting me make that decision.* Sometimes a little tough love and discomfort can save you and your child tens of thousands of dollars! Thanks to this wise decision by my parents, I was fortunate enough to graduate with my accounting degree debt free. (Thanks Mom and Dad!)

Look, I want your children to get an education so they have productive, well-paying careers. I also want to see them graduate with as little student loan debt as possible! It's hard enough to start out your young adult life without being weighed down by a mountain of debt. By following the suggestions in this chapter, you can help your child choose the right major at the right college for the right price.

ACTION ITEMS

Ask yourself the following questions: What is my child's preferred career path? Who can we talk to in this field of work to find out what type of education and training is preferred by employers? What can we do to start saving money for college now? What strategies can we employ to reduce or eliminate the amount of money my child will need to borrow via student loans?

CHAPTER 29

Mastering Your Mortgage

ome, sweet home! Home ownership is woven into the fabric of the American dream. However, if you buy a house the *wrong* way, the results could be a nightmare! This is a tricky subject because our home is the one tangible thing we buy to which almost everyone has an emotional attachment. Our home is where we eat, sleep, and raise our families. It represents a place of comfort and safety, our refuge from the world.

We use the word "home" and "house" interchangeably, but they don't mean the same thing. According to Dictionary.com *home* is "the place in which one's domestic affections are centered; any place of residence or refuge." A house is simply one type of building in which you could make your home. You could also make your home in an apartment, condo, house boat, RV, or tiny house. "Home is where the heart is." You can probably see how this financial transaction, typically the largest purchase most people will make in their lifetimes, can be fraught with emotional landmines.

The most serious problem occurs when we "fall in love" with a house or condo that is beyond our budget. Home ownership will not be a pleasant affair if it causes continual money stress in our lives, no matter how much we love the granite countertops in the kitchen and the Jacuzzi tub on the deck. This is why I want you to master your mortgage so it doesn't master you!

A mortgage is a loan secured by a house (or condo) and land that will typically increase, or at least hold, its value. I say "typically" because if you were a homeowner during the housing bubble of 2007–2009, you likely saw the value of your home drop or stagnate, as I did. However, in general, over the long term, real estate is an asset which appreciates over time. In my opinion, the only "good" type of consumer debt is a mortgage because it's a forced savings plan which builds up equity over time, which isn't the case with renting.

Is it possible to own a home without a mortgage? Yes, it can be done! I've seen a young couple rent a small apartment, live on one income, and save the other income for several years. This strategy enabled them to purchase a small starter home for cash. If you are a young adult just starting out in life, I highly recommend doing this. Even if you're not a spring chicken and currently have a mortgage, paying extra on it each and every month will shave years off of your loan. In fact, almost one-third of homes in America are owned free and clear. I was a little surprised when I learned this fact, because I thought just about everyone had a mortgage!

Most of us are not patient enough to save up cash to buy a house. So, if you are going to get a mortgage to purchase a home, *my advice is to borrow as little as possible and pay it back as quickly as possible.* A general rule of thumb is your mortgage payment, including escrow, should be no more than 30% of your household's take-home pay. However, it's best to look at your entire financial picture, including all of your expenses and debt payments, to see what you're truly able to afford. I'll never forget when Nick and I purchased our current home—my first mortgage—and the loan officer told us we qualified for almost three times the amount we wanted to borrow. If we had a mortgage that big, there's no way we'd be able to afford food and utilities! Rather than asking, "What's the most I can borrow?" Ask, "What's the least I can borrow?"

When you are shopping for a mortgage, you should stick with a fixed-rate loan with reasonable closing costs and make a down payment of at least 20%. Making a down payment of at least 20% will keep you from paying PMI, Private Mortgage Insurance. PMI is foreclosure insurance which protects the bank—not you—in case you default on the loan and the bank can't sell it for enough to cover your outstanding balance. PMI can easily add $100 or more per month to your mortgage payment, which is why I want you to steer clear of it! If you are financing more than 80% of the home's value, PMI is required.

This being said, we still want to pay off the mortgage as quickly as we can, but things need to be done in the proper order. Don't pay extra on your house payment until: all of your other non-mortgage debt is paid in full, you have six months of expenses in your emergency savings, and you're putting 15% of your income into retirement accounts. If you have all of your other debts paid off, you should have a pretty big chunk of change to pay extra on the principal of your home loan.

~

Here are some tips for mastering your mortgage:

- **Always escrow your property taxes and homeowners insurance!** It's much easier to make a slightly larger mortgage payment than to come up with several thousand dollars at once for these annual payments. I've had several clients come to me in serious financial trouble because they didn't escrow their property taxes and homeowners insurance, nor did they set the money aside on a monthly basis to pay them. Big mistake!
- Did you know if you have paid down your mortgage to the point of having at least 20% equity in your home, that the mortgage company cannot require you to pay PMI? You will probably have to pay for a home appraisal out of your pocket to prove there's at least 20% equity, but you'll recoup the money in just a few short months!
- **Your interest rate matters!** If you are applying for a mortgage, your credit score will determine your interest rate, which directly affects your payment. Typically, a

mortgage lender wants to see several sources of credit reported on your credit report in good standing for at least a year or two. Shop around for the best interest rate among several lenders. It may be worth paying slightly higher out-of-pocket closing costs for a lower rate. If you are financing $200,000 for 30 years, the difference in interest paid over the life of the loan from 4.5% to 4% is over $21,000! Even if your closing costs are $2,000 higher to get the 4%, that's a fabulous deal over the life of the loan!

- **You will save massive amounts of money by choosing a 15-year mortgage instead of a 30-year mortgage!** If your mortgage is $200,000 at 4.5%, *you will save a whopping $89,415 in interest* by choosing a 15-year mortgage over a 30-year one. And surprisingly, the payment is not double; it's only 50% higher. ($1,530/ month at 15 years vs. $1,013/ month at 30 years.) Don't believe me? Check it for yourself here: http://www.bankrate.com/calculators/mortgages/mortgage-calculator.aspx

- **Avoid home equity lines of credit (HELOC's) and second mortgages.** Do *not* treat your home like a credit card and use the equity to buy luxuries like vacations, motorcycles, and boats. It's also a bad idea to use your home's equity to consolidate other debt. (More on this in a future chapter.) Your goal is to be debt free so you can pay cash for both your wants and needs. If you overextend your mortgage debt, you could be in danger of foreclosure if you lose your job or have a cut in income.

- **Beware of reverse mortgages!** Reverse mortgages pay you a monthly check, but then you're back into debt on your home. These loans are targeted at seniors and have a tendency to be fraught with high fees. The last thing you want to do is to be back into debt in your golden years.

- Your goal should be mortgage-free by retirement if not sooner!

If you are not yet financially healthy enough to handle a mortgage payment, it's okay to rent! You may have heard people say, "Don't rent! You're just throwing your money away if you do!" I understand the point they are making. Having a mortgage is like a type of savings account, because each month, your equity builds a little at a time. However, if you're going to struggle to make the mortgage payment, renting for a time may be your best option. Maybe you need to spend a year or two hammering on your credit card debt or student loans before home ownership makes financial sense for you. If you are in the military or you have a job where relocation is likely, renting a house or an apartment may be the smartest financial move for your family.

There are several scenarios where renting may be the better option.

If you're not financially healthy, it's the right time to rent. If you're deeply in debt and have very little savings, buying a home would likely bring more money stress your way. We tend to underestimate the additional costs of being a homeowner versus a renter. When you're renting, your landlord pays for the taxes, maintenance, and emergency breakdowns. If you're a homeowner, that's all on you. If you don't have a savings account to take care of fixing or replacing appliances and other upkeep, home ownership is going to stress you out to the max!

If you're in transition, it's the right time to rent. If your life is in transition, purchasing real estate may not be the right move for you at this time. If you're recently divorced, your spouse just passed away, your kids have left for college, or you're in between jobs, renting an apartment, house, or condo may be the best solution for now. The problem with buying and selling a home is the process usually takes time and money. If a newly widowed woman buys a smaller house, then decides a year later to move to another state to be closer to her grandchildren, she's going to have to deal with the expense and stress of selling a house on top of moving. Renting for a year while she processes her grief and figures out her future plans would save her money and effort.

If you like to wander, it's the right time to rent. Owning a home ties you to a specific location. While many people love this fact, there are others who feel stifled by this. If you love to travel and would rather spend your time and money exploring the world, home ownership may not be the right choice for you. If you own a home and spend extensive time traveling for work or pleasure, you'll end up paying someone to ensure your property is cared for while you're gone. Renting a place (or just a room) may be a much better option for those happily afflicted with wanderlust.

If relocation is in your future, it's the right time to rent. If you are in the military or your spouse has a career in which relocation is a reality, buying a home could be a financial disaster for your family. Real estate is generally a good investment in a long run, but buying and then selling a few years later could leave you upside down or in a breakeven situation at best. If you're moving out of state, showing and selling the home while trying to settle into a new military base or new office culture is more stress than anyone needs! What if you are a homeowner preparing to relocate right now? If you're facing a break-even or upside down selling situation, you could elect to turn your house into an income-producing investment, letting a property management company handle the tenants and send you a monthly check.

~

There is a right time to rent and a right time to buy a home; it all depends on your individual financial and family situation. The only debt my husband and I have is our mortgage and we are diligently working on paying it off ahead of schedule. I can't wait for the day when we are completely debt-free!

ACTION ITEMS

Close your eyes and imagine life with NO house payment! What would you do with all that money? Do you have a mortgage?

Are you paying extra on it right now? What steps do you need to take to master your mortgage?

CHAPTER 30

The Underbelly of the Financial World

There are plenty of ways to get into debt, and not all of them are created equally. There are some financial waters so dark and dangerous; no good can come of going there. In this chapter, I expose what I call the "Underbelly of the Financial World:" payday lending, pawning, and overdraft protection loans. Unfortunately, I have first-hand experience battling some of these monsters and have the scars to show for it. My goal is for you to learn from my mistakes.

~

TV shows like Pawn Stars make it seem like pawn shops are all fun and games. However, these programs mainly showcase people selling their cool and unique items. What's the difference between pawning and selling?

Selling is straightforward: we agree on a price, I give the item to the pawn shop and they pay me cash for it. End of story. On the other hand, pawning is essentially taking out a loan against the item. The pawn shop gives me cash and they hold onto the item until I pay them back. However, there's also interest payments involved, which can add up quickly.

CASE STUDY: GRANDMA'S WEDDING RING

My fiancé, Jeff, came to me and told me his best friend, "Brad," had been arrested and was in jail. "Brad didn't do anything wrong! He got in a fight with his girlfriend and she called the cops on him. I have to help him; he's my best friend." (This meant *I* had to help Brad, because Jeff certainly didn't have the money!) I didn't have the cash, but I did own some jewelry that was worth something. So I took my grandmother's wedding ring to the pawn shop. The owner gave me $150 for it on a pawn. I had to pay $30/ month in interest. If I didn't, the pawn shop would have every right to sell it. If I wanted to get it back, I had to repay the original $150, which I could never seem to scrape together. I ended up paying interest on it for 24 months, $720 in total. That's 480% of what I originally borrowed! The pawn shop owner finally took pity on me and gave me back the ring, because I paid on it for so long. In case you're wondering, neither Jeff nor his friend Brad ever paid me back the $150.

Here's the lesson I learned: Pawn shops are a great place to sell things you don't want. But pawning items near and dear to you is costly—both in emotional currency and in real dollars! Don't use a pawn shop to borrow money. It's much smarter to have an emergency fund.

~

Payday lending is the absolute *worst* way to borrow money! Consider these shocking facts regarding payday loans from the Center for Responsible Lending:

- The typical two-week payday loan has an annual interest rate ranging from 391 to 521 percent.
- Nationally, there are more than two payday lending storefronts for every Starbucks location.
- Repeated payday loans result in $3.5 billion in fees each year.

- Payday borrowers are more likely to have credit card delinquency, unpaid medical bills, overdraft fees leading to closed bank accounts, and even bankruptcy.

If payday lenders are so horrible, why does anyone use them? Unfortunately, payday lenders market their "services" to those people with low levels of financial literacy and high levels of desperation. They position themselves as being a friendly resource to help you in your time of need, giving you an advance until your next paycheck. Unfortunately, many folks get caught up in the cycle of repeating payday loans paycheck after paycheck. I know because it happened to me.

Here's how the process generally works. Let's say I want to borrow $500 from a payday lender until my next paycheck. I write the lender a check, not for $500, but for $550 (they are charging me $50, or 10% of the total, to borrow this money for two weeks.) They give me the $500 today and hold my check until payday. However, once payday rolls around and the check for $550 clears, I'm back in the same boat again: not enough money to pay my bills. So, I go back to the payday lender and now I need to borrow $550. I will have to write a check for $605 ($550 + a $55 fee) to get the $550 today. As you can see, this continues to spiral out of control, the amounts getting higher and higher, as time goes on.

By the time I hit financial rock bottom, I owed money to three different payday lenders. Checks started to bounce and overdraft fees began to mount. I ended up having to close my checking account and make arrangements to send each payday lender a certain amount of money each month to pay my debts. The whole situation was a serious black eye to my financial reputation.

~

Overdraft protection loans on your checking account have the potential to turn into the same sort of recurring nightmare. Laziness over balancing our checking accounts deposited $30 billion in bank coffers last year! So it would seem like overdraft protection loans would be a good thing, right?

Quite the contrary. The interest rates can be high and the bank is profiting from your sloppy money habits. I would much rather see my clients keep a cushion of several hundred dollars in their checking accounts and balance them regularly than to have access to overdraft protection loans. It's too easy to overspend, knowing the cushion is there to draw upon.

CASE STUDY: "WE'RE FROM THE BANK, AND WE'RE HERE TO HELP!"

"Denise" was struggling with her bills. A military mom with four young children, it wasn't uncommon for her to overdraw her checking account with debit card transactions. Before his deployment, Denise's husband, Jack, handled most of the family's personal finances. When she met with the branch manager at her local bank to get some assistance with straightening out her account, he said, "We have the perfect solution for you!" It turns out the banker's "solution" was to open a credit card in Denise's name and connect it to her account. If she overdrew her account, the credit card would advance money into the checking account. Instead of teaching Denise how to balance her account, her banker sold her more debt! There was a per-transaction fee each time the card transferred money to her checking account when it went into the red, plus interest on the money borrowed. Because Denise knew the card was there to catch her slack, her spending spiraled out of control to the tune of $14,000. Denise told me, "I thought my banker had my back. Turns out, he had his hand in my wallet."

ACTION ITEMS

Have you borrowed money from any of these shady characters from the "Underbelly of the Financial World?" What was your experience? What actions will you take to ensure you steer clear of these dangerous debt products in the future?

CHAPTER 31

Good Debt, Bad Debt

I s all debt bad? Is it possible to live 100% debt free? Are there times when it may be advisable to take out a loan? Debt is certainly one of the biggest causes of financial distress, but not all debt is the same. You've just learned the ins and outs of different types of debt and the negative repercussions. It's now up to *you* to decide what level of debt your family is comfortable with carrying, if any. As I said earlier, the weight of debt can be very heavy, so I want you to be very cautious with it. I would love for you to avoid debt entirely, however I know that may not be your choice. So if you are going to borrow, keep these two important rules in mind:

1. Borrow as little as possible and pay it back as quickly as possible.
2. Debt should not be used for consumption, only to build income and wealth.

When my husband and I bought our first house together, we were in 100% agreement on rule #1: Borrow as little as possible and pay it back as quickly as possible. We put down as much as we could on the house and regularly pay extra on it when possible. The norm today is putting zero down and stretching payments out as long as the bank will let you! You're going to be like a salmon swimming upstream when you ask the lender how quickly you can pay back your loan. Be sure to inquire when obtaining a mortgage or other loan if there are any prepayment penalties. Some banks try to protect their interest income by penalizing you if you pay off the loan too early. Personally, I would never agree to a loan with a prepayment penalty clause.

"Is it okay to use a credit card if I pay it off in full every month?" Of course it's okay; it's your choice. People do have a tendency to overspend when using credit cards, so you have to honestly ask yourself if you fall into that camp. I know I can't trust myself with a credit card anywhere near a shopping mall! It's why I haven't had one in more than a dozen years. My husband is more of a saver than a spender. When we first started dating, Nick had one credit card he paid in full every month. He is in the small segment of people who are going to spend the same amount of money, no matter what the payment method. For quite a few years, my husband used his debit card exclusively. Just recently, Nick decided he wanted to use a credit card versus a debit card. The tight security features on his debit card (like the $1,000 transaction limit) were too restrictive and causing him some headaches. I know he will use it responsibly and pay it in full every month, which is why I'm okay with it. And there might come a day when I trust myself with one, too.

~

Let's look at the second rule: *Debt should not be used for consumption, only to build income and wealth.* What do I mean by consumption? Anything that diminishes in value as time passes is a "consumable." Some things are consumed immediately, like entertainment and food. Others are consumed over a longer period of time, such as shoes, clothing, and cars. In either case, the value of the item decreases. This is why I don't advocate going into credit card debt for daily living expenses or taking out car loans. You're best served to pay for these things with cash or your debit card.

How would someone use debt to build income or wealth? If you are obtaining a mortgage for a home which increases in value or a loan for a business venture that is going to provide you with positive monthly cash flow, this *may* be a wise money move. I have several friends who invest in rental real estate, and they do use the bank's money to fund at least part of their investments. They do their research to ensure the investment itself is a good one, and then decide how much money they feel comfortable borrowing on the venture. I'm not an investment expert, and I'm not giving a blanket endorsement for investing in real estate. However, if you have the opportunity to purchase an investment or ownership in a business, it may be worth considering taking a loan for the opportunity. It's something you should discuss with your financial advisor, CPA, and/or tax professional. I would much rather see someone borrow money on a cash flow producing four-family apartment building than a luxury car that will go down in value the minute they drive it off of the car dealer's lot.

Both personal and business debts have the potential to spread like a cancer and destroy your financial health. My best advice regarding debt is to avoid it if you can. Be very cautious and conservative with any debt you take on, even if it is for cash producing assets. Make sure you and your spouse are in agreement with any debt you decide to incur.

ACTION ITEMS

Do you consider any type of debt to be "good?" Are you comfortable carrying around the weight of some debt or will you go for the gold and strive to be 100% debt free?

CHAPTER 32

The Right Time to Refinance

Here is a question I'm frequently asked by my coaching clients: "While you are working to pay off your debt, is it ever a good idea to refinance some or all of it to a lower interest rate?"

The answer depends on your particular situation and your mindset. If you are viewing debt consolidation as a magic pill to solve your financial ills, the red flag should go up. There is no quick fix to a mountain of consumer debt. Some people transfer balances between credit cards the way a magician uses sleight of hand to hide the ball under one of three cups. Moving debt from one financial institution to another doesn't fix the underlying problem of overspending. However, if you have a warrior mindset and you want to destroy your debt as quickly as possible, refinancing your debt (if done the right way) can accelerate the process.

My personal experience with consolidation loans wasn't a positive one. I went to one of those shady finance companies located in a strip mall to consolidate my debt, which included store credit cards, bank credit cards, and some minor medical bills. I didn't realize until it was too late that the reason my payment was lower was because the repayment time was stretched out, not because it was a great interest rate. I had thrown no-interest medical bills into the mix and was now paying more than 20% on them. Even worse, a year later I had run up the credit cards again! This meant I had the consolidation loan *plus* the credit card bills. If you are considering a loan like this, be sure to read the fine print and understand the fees and interest rate. Don't put low or no-interest bills into your consolidation loan. Close and cut up the credit cards, so you don't end up in the same mess I did!

A home equity line of credit (HELOC) or a second mortgage may appear to be a great way to pay off your credit cards and other consumer loans. Most HELOC's and second mortgages have nice low rates and the interest is deductible on your tax return. However, I would advise you to proceed with caution before refinancing your home or taking out a second mortgage for the purposes of debt consolidation. What happens if you lose your income for whatever reason and can't pay all of the bills? If you don't pay your credit cards, collectors will scream at you to pay them, but they can't foreclose on your house. If your mortgage payment suddenly becomes unaffordable because you lost your job, you're risking your family's home, not just your credit score.

Do not, under any circumstances, use a 401(k) loan to pay off your debt! The money in your 401(k) is protected from creditors and is for your retirement. When you take out a 401(k) loan, you remove that protection. If you have an outstanding loan and you leave your job for any reason, whether you are laid off or quit, the balance is due in full within *60 days*. If you don't pay the balance back by the deadline, you'll be hit with taxes and penalties. The money you borrow via a 401(k) loan is also unplugged from the investments in your portfolio which means you are missing out on the compounding growth needed to fund your retirement. Borrowing from your 401(k) for debt consolidation is a bad idea all the way around.

Balance transfers between credit cards can potentially accelerate your debt reduction plan. Many banks offer six to twelve months of low or no interest as a teaser to switch to their card. It may not always be the right decision, so be sure to look at the fine print. How long is the low or no interest rate in place? What will be the interest rate after that? The second question is probably more important than the first one. How does the new card's regular rate stack up against what you're currently paying? How much of the balance will you be paying off during the teaser rate period? Don't make the mistake of assuming you'll be able to jump ship and transfer balances again, because you don't know if the opportunity will be there when the time comes.

Here's the bottom line: you can't borrow your way out of debt. The only way to permanently become debt free is to pay more than the minimum due on your credit cards and loans month after month, until they are paid in full. If your end-goal is living debt free, refinancing can fast-track your journey *if* you do it right.

ACTION ITEMS

If you are considering refinancing some of your debt, ask yourself these questions: "What is my motivation for refinancing? Am I committed to being debt free, or am I just looking for an easy way out?"

CHAPTER 33

Your Credit Score is Not a Measure of Financial Success

Americans seem to be obsessed with their credit scores. There are websites and mobile apps to monitor changes in your credit report and credit score and send you alerts. There are commercials on late night TV from companies promising to repair your credit. You may even hear people saying you need to do certain things to *build your credit*. But if you ask people how their credit score is calculated, most of them don't even know.

Essentially, your credit score is calculated based on how you interact with debt. You need to have *some* debt in order to have a credit score. But you can't have too much debt. And you have to "play nice" with the debt you have—making your payments on time—in order to keep your score in the acceptable range.

Here are the factors taken into account when calculating a credit score, and the weight put on each:

- 35% Payment History
- 30% Amounts Owed
- 15% Length of Credit History
- 10% New Credit

- 10% Types of Credit Used

Your credit score does not take into account how much money you have in the bank, whether or not you are employed, how much money you make at your job, or your 401(k) balance. I hope you're beginning to see the limitation of the credit score. It is not the best measure of financial success. Your net worth—which is what you own minus what you owe—is a much better indicator of your financial health. You could inherit a million dollars from your grandmother tomorrow and your credit score will *not* increase even one point because of it.

Some people are obsessed with their credit score in the same way others are obsessed with the number on the scale. Let's imagine that two women we know, Hailey and Alexa, are both 5'5" and weigh 135 pounds. Hailey works out six days a week, drinks protein shakes for breakfast, and generally leads a healthy lifestyle. Alexa smokes a pack of cigarettes a day, eats a donut for breakfast, and goes to the tanning bed several times a week. Of course, we are smart enough to know Hailey is much healthier than Alexa, even though they both weigh 135 pounds. In this very same way, two people can have identical credit scores, but one may have a net worth of $800,000 and the other one may only have a net worth of $8,000. So do *not* obsess over your credit score! It is just one measure of how you're doing financially, and only in relation to your debt.

~

Here are the top questions I'm asked about credit reports and credit scores:

- *"If I'm not going to borrow money, should I even worry about my credit score?"* Although your credit score isn't as significant as you might have previously thought, it's not completely meaningless. Most people aren't in a position to pay cash for their home and your credit report affects your mortgage interest rate. If your score is low, this can cost you some serious money over the life of your mortgage. Even if you don't want to borrow money, your credit score and credit report are used by landlords, insurance companies, and employers as a measure of your financial responsibility.

- *"Why do employers and insurance companies check my credit?"* Credit reports and credit scores are a good indicator of personal responsibility. Studies have demonstrated a direct correlation between a person's credit and the likelihood of him or her filing an insurance claim. Individuals with poor credit history are generally more likely to file car insurance claims, so they will often pay above-average car insurance rates. Three states— California, Massachusetts and Hawaii—currently forbid insurers from using credit data when determining car insurance rates, but other states allow it to some degree. Employers check credit especially when potential employees will have access to company credit cards and other assets.

- *"How often should I pull my credit report and check my credit score?"* You should pull your credit report at least once a year to make sure there aren't any errors on it that could be hurting your rating, and to check for identity theft. You can do this for free at AnnualCreditReport.com.

- *"How can I improve my credit score if it's not very good?"* Becoming financially healthy will naturally improve your score, just as improving your physical health will bring your body weight into a healthier range. Close your credit cards as you pay them off with your debt reduction plan, not all at once. Your credit score will take a dive if you close multiple accounts at once. I advise my coaching clients to close their accounts as they pay them down to zero. If there is any erroneous information on your credit report, you will need to take steps to correct it or get it removed. You can do this by going directly to the three credit reporting agencies' websites (Equifax, TransUnion, and Experian.) There are a myriad of factors that can affect your credit score, and it can be a little confusing to say the least. For more detailed information, go to MyFICO.com.

- *"If I have a low credit score, should I hire someone for credit repair?"* Absolutely not! You can do this yourself by becoming financially healthy, systematically paying down your debts, and communicating with the credit reporting agencies. It does take some time and effort to check your credit report and dispute errors, but it's rarely worth the price to hire someone else to do it for you.

- *"Should I purchase identity theft protection?"* Yes, you should, because every 2 seconds someone's identity is stolen! It could take you hundreds of hours to clean up the mess and clear your name, even though you're not at fault. Be sure to purchase the *right kind* of identity theft protection. You want one with credit recovery/restoration services, not just credit monitoring. Be sure to cover your entire family, including your children. Identity theft perpetrated with a child's social security number is skyrocketing, so you want to protect their future credit histories as well. Shop around among a few providers to find the best deal for the coverage you need. Currently, I'm paying less than $15 per month to cover both my husband and me.

- *"How do I maintain a good credit score with little or no debt?"* If you just have a mortgage, you likely don't need credit cards or other outstanding loans to maintain a great credit score. My husband and I haven't had credit cards in more than a dozen years, and we both have excellent credit ratings. The only debt we have is our mortgage.

- *"What if my house is paid in full?"* If you don't have a mortgage, a secured credit card is a great option. Here's an example of how it works. You go to your local bank and open a savings account with $1,000. The bank puts a freeze on the money and issues you a credit card with a $1,000 limit. You use the credit card for a few things, like gas for your car, and then pay it in full each month. If you ever get into financial trouble, you can have the bank use the savings account to pay off the card and close it. You don't run the risk of racking up debt you can't pay back. Secured credit cards are reported to the credit bureau just the same as a regular credit card. This is a great way for college students to build their credit, so they'll be able to rent an apartment or buy a house later on.

- *"What is a Credit Builder Loan?"* A good alternative to a secured credit card is the credit builder loan, offered by many credit unions and some banks. Here's how they work. You agree to pay them a certain amount every month, say $100 per month for 24 months. When you pay them the $100, the bank or credit union puts it into a savings account for you and reports your on-time "payment" to the credit reporting agencies. At the end of the term, you have a nice little nest egg that is returned to you and can be used to pad your emergency fund or as a down payment for a home purchase. You do pay the bank a small monthly fee for this "loan," but it's certainly preferable to credit card debt, in my opinion.

Resolve to become more mindful of your net worth than your credit score. If you focus on being financially healthy, your credit score will largely take care of itself.

ACTION ITEMS

Ask yourself the following questions: "Am I obsessed with my credit score? If so, why? What is my net worth?" If you haven't pulled your credit report in the last year, go to AnnualCreditReport.com and do it now.

CHAPTER 34

Your Debt Reduction Plan

Now that you know the ins and outs of debt and the benefits of living debt free, it's finally time to start working on your debt reduction plan. Before we dive in to the specifics, there are a few prerequisites to be checked off your list. First and foremost, you must have your spending plan—the budget—in place. If you don't have control over your monthly spending, it's going to be very hard to systematically pay down your debt.

Before you begin paying extra on your debt, you should have a small emergency fund in place. I recommend at least one month's worth of your living expenses; this amount will come directly from your budget. The reason you do this first before attacking your debt is so you don't have to charge your emergencies on a credit card when they happen. And they will happen! If you have a car repair, medical bill, or other unexpected expense, you'll have a small cushion of cash in your savings account to pay for it.

You must *stop* borrowing money. You cannot get out of this mess by continuing your current behavior. Cut up those credit cards or put them on ice, literally! In the meantime, use cash, debit cards, or pre-paid credit cards for your monthly expenditures.

There are several methods for accelerating your debt reduction plan. The first and most popular is the "debt snowball." Very simply, here is how the debt snowball works. Make a list of your debts from the smallest balance to the largest. Add up all of your minimum monthly payments. You are going to make the minimum payment on all of your debts, except for the smallest one. You are going to find every extra dollar you possibly can and pay it on the little one. Attack it with a vengeance! Once the smallest debt is paid off, you apply the amount you used to pay on it towards the second smallest one, in addition to the minimum payment. When the second debt is paid off, you apply the old monthly payments from debt #1 and debt #2 onto debt #3. By the time you reach the larger debts on your list like student loans and car payments, you'll be making double or triple payments on them monthly, which will pay them off at lightning speed.

Why is the debt snowball my preferred method for debt reduction for my coaching clients? Wouldn't it be financially smarter to pay the one with the highest interest rate first? Well, if money was just about math, none of us would have credit card debt. We'd crunch the numbers and realize what a bad idea it is. Money is emotional! It's the reason why we're in debt in the first place. The debt snowball harnesses our positive emotions and uses them to propel us towards success. When we attack our smallest debt with a vengeance, we achieve a quick victory, and it keeps us pumped up. Our monthly pile of bills starts to shrink and we feel encouraged to stick with the process. If, like me, you enjoy crossing things off the list, the debt snowball method is the choice for you.

One alternative to the debt snowball is the Annual Percentage Method (also called the "debt stacking method," or the "debt avalanche method.") The annual percentage method is identical to the debt snowball, with one exception. You list your debts in order of interest rate, from largest to smallest. You put any extra money you can come up with on the debt with the largest interest rate. (The payoff balances are irrelevant with this method.) Once the debt is paid off, you move on to the debt with the second highest interest rate. If you are more motivated by how much interest you're saving instead of how many bills are in your stack, this method may be best suited for you.

The final alternative for debt reduction is the Proportional Method, or as I call it the "fair share approach." You divide your extra cash for paying debt proportionally among your bills. For example, let's say you have $200 above and beyond your minimum monthly payments available for debt reduction. One of your credit card bills represents 10% of your total debt. You would add $20 (10% of the $200) to the monthly payment. This method requires more number crunching and can be confusing for those who don't like math. However, if fairness is important to you and you want to ensure all of your creditors get paid a little extra every month, this approach may be right for you.

If you really want to gain some traction and accelerate your debt reduction plan, you'll need to find some ways to make extra cash. Is overtime available at your current job? Are you able to work a second job, part time on the weekends? I'm not suggesting you work overtime or two jobs for the rest of your life—just until you've paid down enough debt to get some breathing room. Maybe you can monetize a hobby, such as photography, pet sitting, or freelance writing. Take all those coffee cans of loose change to the bank and make an extra payment on your credit card. Sell some stuff! Most of us have so much junk we don't even know what half of it is. Have a yard sale, take your old clothes to a consignment shop, and sell some things on E-Bay or Craigslist.

ACTION ITEMS

Answer the following questions: What are your thoughts about putting your debt reduction plan into action? Which debt reduction method appeals to you most: the debt snowball, the annual percentage method, or the fair share method? What is one thing you can do today to begin?

CHAPTER 35

What's Your Fight Song?

Are you ready to draw a line in the sand and decide once and for all that your debt is going down? Are you sick and tired of being weighed down by the heavy burden of debt? If you are at the point where you exclaim, "I've had it! I'm done living like this! I can't take it anymore!" then congratulations! You are ready to tackle the challenge of paying off your debt once and for all. At first it's going to seem hard and progress will be slow, so expect it. Your debt-destroying muscles are small and wimpy at the beginning. You wouldn't walk into the gym your first day and start lifting 200 pounds. It's the same with building your financial muscles. This is why I tell people to pay their smallest bill off first and work their way up to the bigger ones.

There are two things you need to successfully conquer your debt: a plan and a warrior mentality. Your plan consists of your Financial Roadmap, including your budget and debt reduction plan. Your budget will keep spending on track so you don't go further into debt. Your debt reduction plan will set your priorities regarding which debt to attack first.

The second thing you need for success is a *warrior mentality*. You need to attack your debt with a vengeance and show no mercy. Debt is not your friend! It is stealing your paycheck! Get fired up! It's you vs. debt, in the ultimate cage match. I'm a huge fan of mixed martial arts (MMA). And if you have ever watched an MMA fight or a boxing match, you'll notice something interesting if you pay attention to the fighters. When they walk out to the cage or the ring, their fight song is blaring and they have this look of fierce determination on their faces. That fighter *knows* he's going to win deep down in his heart. You can see it in his body language. You must to have this same kind of conviction. In fact, I want you to pick your fight song. And when you feel your motivation draining away, blare it loud enough for the neighbors to hear!

Keep in mind that success is not a straight line, so don't give up! Sometimes a fighter will lose the first two rounds on the scorecards but win the fight via knockout or submission in the final round. There will be setbacks and detours on your journey to becoming debt free. However, *the only way you will fail is if you give up*. Even prize fighters lose a match from time to time. What differentiates a champion is that he gets back up, dusts himself off, and gets back in the ring. I promise you, once you experience the freedom and lightness of being debt free, you'll never, ever want to go back!

Be sure to celebrate your victories along the way! When you have paid off a credit card or student loan, do something entertaining and memorable to mark the special occasion. When a fighter wins a big match, he goes out to eat, drink, and celebrate with his friends and family. Just make sure your reward doesn't wipe out your progress.

ACTION ITEMS

Ask yourself these questions: "Am I sick and tired of being weighed down by debt? Am I willing to put in the hard work of implementing my debt reduction plan? How can I achieve and keep a warrior mentality? What will be my 'fight song' to fire me up when my motivation is slipping?"

PART FOUR

Emotionally Charged Saving

CHAPTER 36

The Sad State of Our Savings

We are not good savers here in America. At one time, we used to be, but not anymore. We not only spend everything we make, we frequently go into debt to buy more, more, more. As we learned in the previous section, debt is the enemy of saving and investing. I recently had the privilege of hearing Daymond John, the founder of FUBU and one of the stars on Shark Tank, speak at the Unpolished Conference in Cincinnati. He said something so simple, yet so profound about personal finance: "Your assets feed you; your liabilities eat you." Debt eats away at your income, which makes it very hard to save. That's why we must first attack our debt with a vengeance so we can save and invest.

Many people don't even have a modest amount saved to cover unexpected expenses. According to a survey done by GoBankingRates.com in 2015, 62% of Americans have less than $1,000 in savings. 21% of respondents didn't even have a savings account! Only 14% had more than $10,000 in savings which is only two to three months of living expenses for most families. Our savings accounts are dangerously anemic!

Why don't we save more? I think part of the reason is our consumer driven culture. We're constantly bombarded by advertisements reminding us how deficient we are unless we own this or that product. It's vitally important we become mindful of our spending habits so we have money to save and invest. The other reason we don't save is because we don't make it a priority. If saving isn't important to us, we won't do it. I'm going to show you how to wield the power of emotion to super charge your motivation to save and invest for your future.

ACTION ITEMS

How much money do you currently have in savings? What do you think is holding you back from saving more: a lack of desire, too much debt, or both?

CHAPTER 37

Financial Shock Absorbers

There are three main reasons to save money: for emergencies, purchases, and wealth building. The first and most important reason to save is for emergencies. Socking money away for emergencies seems boring, so for most of us it's not a high priority. This is a bad idea! It's the financial equivalent of driving a car without shock absorbers. If you've had the experience of riding in a car with failing shock absorbers, you know whenever you hit a bump or a pothole it's extremely jarring.

When you are on your financial journey with no emergency savings, you will be painfully aware of each and every problem that arises. An emergency fund puts a shock absorber between you and life's expensive problems. Let's say you have an unexpected hospital bill, an urgent home repair, or a broken down vehicle. If you have no emergency savings to pay for the situation, you now have two problems: your original problem *plus* a money problem!

Before I hit financial rock bottom, this was always the case for me. In fact, the reason I borrowed money from those payday lenders started with a car repair bill. If I would have had even just $500 in my savings account, I could have avoided the whole mess! Not only did I have to figure out how I was going to get to and from work while my car was being repaired, but I also had to figure out where to get the money to pay for it. Because I now have an emergency fund, if my car breaks down, I only have a transportation issue. I don't enjoy paying for car repairs, but now I'm just inconvenienced rather than massively stressed out. Now that I have an emergency fund, it seems like I have less emergencies.

How much money should you have in your emergency savings fund? For starters, you should have at least one month's worth of your household expenses. This is the first money goal I set for my coaching clients if their savings balance falls below that amount. This means you must do a budget to know what this amount is in the first place! For the majority of my clients, this falls into the range of $2,500 to $6,000. All of the extra money they are able to trim from their budget goes here first, before paying down debt. It's hard to cut up your credit cards if you don't have a small emergency fund in place.

Once my clients have at least one month's worth of expenses in their emergency fund, we then attack their high interest debt, via their debt reduction plan. After this is accomplished, their goal is to get their emergency fund balance to six months of living expenses. This will ensure the family will be okay financially if there is a medical issue, job loss, or other money crisis.

If you or your spouse is self-employed or on straight commission, the amounts go up. When I decided I wanted to quit my full-time job with the family business and become self-employed, Nick and I made sure we had a big, fat savings cushion before I made the leap. For the self-employed, I generally recommend three months of expenses in your "starter" emergency fund with a goal to ultimately have twelve months of expenses covered in the account. If you are utilizing the Personal Sweep Account discussed in the chapter on variable income, then six months may be sufficient in your emergency fund.

These amounts are not set in stone, so if you're not comfortable only having six months' worth of expenses in your emergency savings, it's certainly okay to save more. In fact, many of my coaching clients feel more at ease having three months of expenses in their savings account before hammering on their debt. If this decreases their stress and makes it easier for them to sleep at night, I'm all for it.

What if you don't currently have an emergency fund? How do you get started? It's very simple: begin systematically putting aside at least a small amount every pay period into a savings account. It's easy to automate this either through your employer or with your bank. Your big goal should be at least six months' worth of your living expenses in your emergency savings. This way, when you hit a financial bump in the road, it won't be quite so painful.

ACTION ITEMS

Open a separate savings account for emergencies and start funding it. Calculate the amounts for your starter emergency fund (one to three months) and your fully padded fund (six months or more). How much will you be transferring per pay period?

CHAPTER 38

Save Up and Pay for It

The second reason to save is for the purchases we wish to make: vacations, clothes, sporting tickets, cars, and other "toys." I've already discussed the pain of financing these purchases with debt: namely overspending and interest payments. In addition to avoiding these negative consequences, there are additional benefits to saving up and paying cash for things.

The first benefit is you're more discriminating with your purchases. When you patiently and persistently save money over time, you are more careful when the time comes to spend it. Chances are, you'll scrutinize your purchases and ensure you're getting exactly what you want. If you've saved up several thousand dollars for a Hawaiian vacation, you're likely to pay close attention to the details of your trip and ensure you're only paying for the amenities you want. If you and your spouse are active and adventurous, you may decide you'd rather spend your money on surfing lessons and scuba excursions instead of paying $100 per night extra to have an ocean front room. If you were putting the vacation on a credit card, you might just do both because you never stopped to consider what was *really* important to you and how much it cost.

When you save up and pay cash, you're more likely to receive a better deal. *Patient people always get better deals than those who are in a buying frenzy.* Saving up over a period of weeks or months gives you time to shop around and locate the best deal on whatever you are looking to buy, whether it's a new pair of leather boots or a used car. If you require financing, it will limit your options to retailers who will approve your credit, and you'll likely overpay for the "privilege." I've recently seen an uptick in the retail establishments, especially restaurants, advertising discounts just for paying with cash instead of credit. I negotiated great deals on the past two cars I've owned because I paid cash for them and wasn't held hostage to dealer financing.

I find I enjoy my purchases more now that I am not going into debt for them. Have you ever bought something you initially loved, but then grew to resent it later because of the debt that came with it? I certainly had my share of retail regret before I hit financial rock bottom. Because I am paying for my purchases with my hard-earned cash, I'm more mindful of what I buy. Now I tend to savor and enjoy the things I choose to buy, and I also take better care of them. The best part is there's no residue of regret clinging to those purchases.

Saving up and paying for your next vacation, car, or latest gadget is pretty simple. Do your research on the approximate cost and divide it by the number of pay periods in between now and when you're going to buy it. Let's say I have my eye on a new laptop costing $800, and I get paid bi-weekly. If I want to purchase it within 4 months, I will need to set aside $100 per pay period in order to buy it. You may even want to open a separate savings account for big goal purchases like a car, and set up automatic transfers to make the process painless.

ACTION ITEMS

What things or experiences do you need to start saving for? How much will you need to set aside each pay period in order to do this?

CHAPTER 39

Investing in Your Future

The final reason to save money is so it can be invested for growth to provide us with income in retirement and funds for our children's college expenses. Saving and investing are similar, yet not quite the same thing. Saved money is usually kept in accounts that are readily available (liquid), FDIC insured, and are earmarked for spending in the relatively near future. Invested money is housed inside of IRAs, 401(k)s and brokerage accounts that are not easily accessible, have more volatility, and won't be spent for five, ten, or even twenty plus years. (Disclaimer: I am neither a financial planner nor an investment professional, and my intent here is not to teach you how to invest your money for retirement. My goal is to teach you *why* you need to invest, and to get you excited about the future.)

Retirement statistics are pretty scary:

- 38% of Americans don't have anything saved for retirement.
- One third of Americans over the age of 65 rely completely on Social Security as their primary source of income.
- Just 14% of American workers are very confident they will have enough money to live comfortably in retirement.

Motivating ourselves to start investing and keep investing is our biggest challenge, and we can blame at least part of it on biology. Homo sapiens are hard wired to choose a certain gain today over a possible gain in the future, even if the latter reward is much greater. Why? Back in our caveman days, our ancestors were running from saber-toothed tigers and scavenging for food. If they wanted to survive, our ancestors had to prioritize success and survival *today* so they would make it to tomorrow. Fortunately, there are some tricks we can use to override the primitive part of our brains and invest for the future.

As with our savings, automating our investing is an excellent idea. If our investments are coming straight off the top of our paycheck into our 401(k) or automatically out of our checking account and into our brokerage account each month, we're more likely to invest consistently. We're actually using our tendency to be lazy in our favor. Once the automatic withdrawals are set up, we're typically too apathetic to cancel or decrease them unless we have a major financial crisis. Out of sight, out of mind! Making regular contributions over a long period of time is the recipe for retirement success. So no matter what age you are, get started right now!

Employers are introducing some cool initiatives to help us save more for retirement. Many businesses are using auto-enrollment into their 401(k) plan with a percentage that captures the entire company match as soon as employees are eligible to participate. Some plans even automatically nudge up the percentage you contribute every year. "Save More Tomorrow" plans, which increase your 401(k) contribution only when you get a raise, are growing in popularity. Of course, you can opt out of any of these automatic increases, but I hope you won't because they are painless ways to ramp up your investing.

Another way to light a fire under your tushie to invest for your future is to picture your elderly self. There are websites, like In20Years.com or FaceRetirement.MerrillEdge.com, which will age a picture of "current you" to see what you'll look like in your golden years. You might find it a little unnerving to see your elderly self, but that's the point. I hope when you look at "future you," you'll have some compassion and want to take care of him or her as you would your elderly parent or grandparent. Think of how you want life to be like for elderly you. Do you want to be zipping around your golf course community in south Florida or stuck in a government-funded retirement home? Print a picture of elderly you to put on your vision board and vow to make good investment decisions *right now*.

~

It's vitally important you have a basic understanding of retirement accounts and the investments (stocks, bonds, mutual funds, ETFs) you hold in them. No, this doesn't have to become a part-time job, but you must educate yourself so you make wise investment decisions. Too many of us rely solely on our financial advisor or our company's 401(k) rep to make decisions for us. This is a bad idea because many are being paid commissions to sell you these investments. Some advisors are truly making the best decision for you and your family, but just as many are choosing the investments that best increase *their* bottom line. If you don't know enough to question their recommendations, you're in danger of being taken to the cleaners. Need a basic education on this subject? I recommend reading or listening to both *Money: Master the Game, 7 Steps to Financial Freedom* by Tony Robbins (I've read it three times!) and *Retire Inspired: It's Not an Age, It's a Financial Number* by Chris Hogan.

Here are some investing questions I'm frequently asked by my coaching clients:

Should I invest while I'm paying off debt? Unless cash flow is super tight or you are in a collections situation, my answer is yes. In my opinion, you should contribute the amount needed to capture the full benefit of your employer's 401(k) match even while you're paying off debt. This is *free money* flowing into your retirement account and I don't want you to miss out on it.

How much should I invest? Generally, you want to be investing at least 10–15% of your income for retirement. Your financial advisor will assist you with coming up with the proper amount to invest, because he or she will take into account your whole financial picture. Once your consumer debt is paid in full, I recommend maxing out both your 401(k)s and IRAs.

What should I invest in? Again, a wise financial advisor will assist you in determining your risk tolerance and growth needs, and will suggest an allocation between various types of investments. It's important to have a working knowledge of the investments you are buying and the associated costs. If you can't explain your investment to a fifth grader, then you don't understand it well enough yourself. If you have been auto-enrolled into your company's 401(k) plan, be sure to meet with the advisor to select your funds. The auto-selected funds may not be the best options for you.

How should I choose my financial planner/investment advisor? Too many of us fall into the trap of selecting an advisor because we know and like them. They are a friend, relative, or someone we know from church. It's not a bad idea to ask the financially healthy people in our lives for recommendations, but be sure to do your own research. Find out how long they have been in the business and how they are getting paid to manage your investments. Personally, I prefer independent advisors because they charge a flat percentage of your assets (typically 1% or less per year) for their fee rather than receiving commissions from mutual fund companies for selling you their investments. Interview two or three advisors, and ask to speak with one or two of their current clients before making your choice. You want an advisor who has the patience to explain investing in a way you can understand. If you feel confused, move on to someone else. Finally, be sure *both* you and your spouse or partner are comfortable with your financial advisor.

ACTION ITEMS

If you are not contributing to your retirement account, begin doing so right away. Meet with your financial advisor at least once a year to review your investments and make sure you are on track for retirement. If you're not happy with your current advisor, ask for recommendations and interview at least two people before making a change. Read or listen to at least one book on investing for retirement.

CHAPTER 40

Saving Equals Deferred Spending

Most people view saving as the opposite of spending, but they are actually two sides to the same coin. Think about it: why do we save money in the first place? It's so we have it available to spend when we need it later. The only difference between saving and spending is time. "Spending" is money we are using now. "Saving" is money we are going to use later. However, many folks approach saving money as something they are *never* going to spend. It's amazing how this little shift in mindset can really motivate you to make saving for the future a priority.

Saving money becomes especially fun and exciting when we think about *how* we're going to spend the money later. If someone is saving money for a new car or a cruise, I recommend they put images of exactly what they want on their vision board. Take a picture of the exact make, model, and color of the car you're saving up for and put it where you'll see it every day. Find pictures of cruise ships and your final destination, and plaster them all over your refrigerator. It makes it exciting rather than painful to make those weekly transfers to your savings account, knowing what you're going to spend it on later.

This same thinking can be applied to the other reasons we want to save money. Even if your retirement is twenty plus years away, dream about where you might like to retire and the activities you'll enjoy doing. Imagine which universities your brilliant children may attend and the satisfied feeling you'll have knowing they won't go into debt for their education.

The least glamourous reason to save is for emergencies. I will admit, it is hard to be excited about it. However, sometimes avoiding negative situations can be as powerful a motivator as embracing positive ones. Think about the last time you had emergencies with financial consequences. How did you feel? Before I had an emergency fund, I would go off the deep end emotionally when financial emergencies happened to me. Now, imagine how it would feel knowing there is plenty of money in your emergency fund for things like car repairs, home maintenance, or unexpected medical bills. You might still be annoyed at the expense and inconvenience, but the situation will surely be less stressful.

By viewing savings as money we get to (mostly) enjoy spending later, instead of never, it makes the habit of saving more appealing and you may find it to be addictive, in a good way!

ACTION ITEMS

What goals are you going to start saving towards now, so you can enjoy them later? Put pictures of these goals on your Financial Vision Board.

CHAPTER 41

Emotionally Charged Saving

Why don't people save more? It's easy to forget about transferring some of your paycheck to savings. It's more fun to spend now than save for later. It's just not important to us. If we really want to ramp up our savings and increase our financial health, we need to have a *burning desire* to save. We can get this burning desire through what I call "Emotionally Charged Saving."

Did you know humans are hardwired to avoid pain and unpleasantness? Avoiding pain is actually a *greater* force for motivation than embracing pleasant situations. Fear is a primal, and often irrational, emotion. Many of us experience some form of fear surrounding money issues, and it can hold us back from being financially healthy. But did you know our money fears can be harnessed to move us toward positive change?

The best way to fuel a burning desire to change our financial behavior is with *both* positive and negative emotions. Certain people are very goal oriented and respond well to positive motivation, which is why I have my coaching clients make Financial Vision Boards with pictures of their savings goals. And others are more motivated by avoiding negative consequences.

We can easily see how negative emotions and experiences cause people to change their physical health. Think of the middle-aged man you know, who for years ate and drank like a college frat boy… that is, until he had a cancer scare or near-fatal stroke. Turning on a dime, this man is now preaching the gospel of good nutrition and running marathons on weekends. The promises of good health, better sleep, and fewer aches and pains weren't enough to motivate this man to take care of himself. It wasn't until he was "scared straight" by a health crisis that he was driven to change his ways. Unfortunately, many of us are this way with our finances. We can use a similar technique in the area of money, *without* having a financial heart attack.

With a little help from our imaginations, we can produce this same force to transform our finances. You see, our brains cannot differentiate between *actual* events that happen to us and events we vividly imagine in our minds. The imagination is a powerful force we can use as a sort of rocket booster to propel us towards our Preferred Financial Future. When we can imagine both the positive benefit of our savings goals and the negative consequences of not achieving them, the result is Emotionally Charged Saving.

Here's an example of how we can emotionally charge one of our savings goals. I would love to retire to Maui. Nick and I have vacationed there twice and adore everything about the island: the beaches, the golf courses, and of course, the perfect weather. We've put pictures of the type of house we'd like to live in on our vision board. We have pictures of the beaches and golf courses on Maui. This gives us a warm fuzzy feeling whenever we see our Financial Vision Board. But is it enough to ensure we're going to make saving for retirement a priority above spending the money now?

Let's add fuel to the emotional fire by imaging how life in retirement will be if we *don't* achieve our savings goals. Now Nick and I will have to remain in our current home, or even downsize to a smaller home. We won't be able to move to Maui, so we'll be facing harsh winters with bad driving conditions. (I hate the cold and snow, so this makes me very depressed because I'd much rather be sitting in the sand sipping a tropical drink with a tiny umbrella.) We won't have any money to take our nieces and nephews on vacation or help with their college expenses. We might even have to go into a government-funded nursing home because of our failing health. We let our imaginations go wild with how horrible it will be to fail at achieving the retirement we want. We could even visit a local nursing home for low-income residents, bringing some balloons or flowers to cheer them up. While we're there, we'll really take in the sights, sounds, and smells to cement the unpleasant image in our minds. By making the contrast of the upside of achieving our savings goal *and* the downside of failing to reach it as sharp as possible, we'll maximize the emotional charge.

Here is the bottom line: if your savings goals are emotionally charged, you are more likely to achieve them. You must have a burning desire to save for the things that are important to you. If you're not excited about your savings goals, then you don't have a big enough reason to change your behavior. If you are finding your money goals and vision board are not giving you the motivational traction you need to make positive changes to your personal finances, consider adding some *negative emotion* to the equation. By making the contrast of the upside of achieving your money goal and the downside of failing to reach it as sharp as possible, you'll maximize the emotional charge and achieve massive motivation. Emotionally charged savings beats discipline and willpower every time.

ACTION ITEM

Select one of your saving goals and emotionally charge it. Vividly imagine both the positives of achieving it and the negatives of failure to attain it.

CHAPTER 42

Mindless Saving

C ommon sense tells us that mindless spending will wreak havoc on our wallets. On the flip side, mindless saving has the potential to grow our bottom line exponentially over time. What do I mean by "mindless saving?" It's setting up your saving habits on auto-pilot, so you don't have to think about them very often.

Our attention is pulled in a thousand directions daily. If we wait until it crosses our minds to transfer money from our checking into our savings accounts, it may never happen. By setting up automatic transfers to happen weekly, bi-weekly, or monthly, the saving habit happens without any effort from us. The only effort expended is the initial set up of the recurring transaction, which is minimal. My husband and I are big fans of "mindless saving." We have automatic transfers set up between our checking and savings accounts to sweep money every pay period into savings. Even though these transfers happen 52 times per year, I only had to set it up once.

Let's say your paycheck is deposited every two weeks into your checking account, and you'd like to save $100 every payday. You could ask your company's payroll department to split-deposit your check for you and put $100 into your savings, which most employers are happy to do. The other option would be to set up a recurring automatic transfer between your accounts at your bank, which can be done online. Rather than transferring the money every two weeks manually, 26 times a year, you only have to do this set up once. And, after the course of a year, you'll have $2,600 in your savings account! You can even download apps for your smart phone, like Acorns, that will round up your purchases and put the extra into a savings or investment account. Some banks have similar programs, such as Bank of America's "Keep the Change® Savings Program."

I highly recommend automating positive money habits like saving for emergencies and investing for retirement. By nature, we humans can be prone to sloppy, lazy money habits and this short circuits that tendency. The biggest objection I receive from this suggestion is, "But what if I end up needing the money for bills this week?" It's pretty simple to transfer it back to your checking account if you *really* need it. But chances are you won't even miss it.

Action Item

Looking at your budget, decide how much money you are going to transfer into your savings account every pay period. Set up the automatic transfer with your bank or employer.

CHAPTER 43

Don't Rob Your Retirement

It kills me when I hear a financial expert recommend borrowing from a 401(k). This mindset has led to many people treating their 401(k)s like a personal ATM. Why is it a bad idea to withdraw cash via a 401(k) loan from your retirement to pay for things like your kids' college, home improvement projects, a vacation, or pay off debt? You're essentially robbing from your future self and your retirement when you do this.

Borrowing from your 401(k) is triple trouble:

1. **You now have a loan payment being directly withdrawn from your paycheck.** Because you're bringing home less every pay period, it's likely you'll be tempted to decrease your contribution during this time, meaning less funds when you retire.
2. **Your loan amount is now unplugged from your chosen investments and therefore not earning an increase.** Yes, you are "paying" yourself interest, but it's usually *much less* than you'd earn over the long haul with your stocks, bonds, and mutual funds.
3. **If you leave your job—voluntarily or involuntarily—the loan amount is due IN FULL within 60 days or taxes and penalties will be due.** The last thing you need

when you're out of work off is a huge payment due or a tax bill.

In addition, your 401(k) account offers important protection to the money inside of it. *401(k) funds are exempt from bankruptcy and untouchable by bill collectors.* Why would you want to pull the money out and expose it to these dangers?

Save up cash for your major purchases and utilize one of the debt reduction techniques we discussed in the Living Debt Free section to pay off your non-mortgage loans. *Never* borrow from your 401(k) or make withdrawals from it to pay for college expenses! There are plenty of ways to cut college expenses and your child can take out student loans if absolutely necessary. However, there is no such thing as a "retirement loan" for you to pay for expenses in your golden years. Remember the picture of "elder you" that you put on your vision board? Imagine an armed robber holding elder you at gun point and stealing his or her money. Guess what? If you are taking out a 401(k) loan, the armed robber is *you.*

~

Although it's not quite as bad as robbing your 401(k), there is an epidemic of neglect which happens when people change jobs. They move on to a new place of employment and forget to take their company 401(k) with them. *When you leave a job, take your 401(k) with you!* What happens when you leave your account behind? It still belongs to you, but it could be transferred to another bank or brokerage account and stuffed into a money market account, earning an anemic rate of return.

I see this scenario on a regular basis with my coaching clients. They have two or three old 401(k)s with previous employers and have no clue how to even access the accounts. I refer them to an investment advisor who helps my clients to transfer and consolidate the old 401(k)s into one actively managed IRA.

*Give your orphaned 401(k) a new home by **directly transferring** it into an IRA with a financial planner.* You can get

167

this paperwork from the HR department of your previous employer. The best time to do this is on your way out the door! By transferring this money to an IRA, you have more control and more investment options than if you leave it with your previous employer's plan. Just be sure to do a *direct transfer* so you're not hit with a tax penalty. Your investment advisor can assist you with this.

ACTION ITEMS

Do you have a 401(k) loan? If so, make a plan to pay it off as soon as possible, and don't rob your retirement again! If you have orphaned 401(k) accounts, make an appointment with your financial advisor and get them rolled over into an IRA so they can be actively managed going forward.

CHAPTER 44

Insurance, Death & Taxes

W hat financial topics do most of us avoid like the plague? Answer: insurance, death, and taxes. We consider these topics to be boring, morbid, and confusing. However, if we ignore these three elephants in our financial room, they could stomp our dreams for money success into oblivion. I promise to make this section short, sweet, and to the point.

~

Insurance is like a financial force field, protecting us from catastrophes. It shields your hard-earned nest egg and ensures your financial health is preserved. It's something no one likes to spend money on, however the right types of insurance are an important part of our financial plan. We have our savings to take care of smaller emergencies, but insurance is there to cover the enormous emergencies we can't pay for ourselves. Here are the types of insurance you should consider owning:

- If you own a home or rent an apartment, **homeowners** or **renters** insurance is essential to protect your house and belongings.
- **Auto**, motorcycle, and boat insurance cover our vehicles and toys.

- **Health** insurance is now required by law and is usually obtained through your employer.
- The purpose of life insurance is to replace income for our spouse and/or children in the event of our passing. The rule of thumb is to have at least 10 times your annual income in **term life** insurance if you have dependents and a mortgage.
- **Personal Liability/ Umbrella** policies protect your assets if you are sued because of an injury on your property or an auto accident. The more wealth you build, the more important this coverage becomes.
- **Disability** insurance pays you a portion of your salary if you are unable to work due to a physical injury or illness.
- **Long Term Care** insurance, also referred to as "nursing home insurance," pays for care in assisted living facilities.
- **Identity Theft** insurance cleans up and restores your credit if you've had it stolen. Identity theft is skyrocketing, so I personally consider this a must.

Some of these insurance policies can be purchased most efficiently through your employee benefit plan at work. Many of my coaching clients don't even know what types of insurance coverages they have available to them from their employer, so it's important to find out. Work with your financial coach or advisor to determine what gaps you have and shop around for a good insurance agent and get yourself covered. I don't want you to overpay for insurance, but don't skimp on what's required to be properly protected. The last thing you need is to experience a tornado ripping through your house, a cancer diagnoses, or a car accident to expose your lack of proper insurance coverage. Get your "financial force field" in place so you know your family will be protected should the unthinkable happen.

~

Considering what will happen to our loved ones' finances when we die is seen as morbid. However, it is actually the most loving thing we can do for our family. According to LexisNexis, approximately 55 percent of Americans do not have a will or estate plan in place. Estate planning, as the lawyers call it, is simply having a legal written plan for the transfer of our wealth when we die.

Many people mistakenly believe estate planning is only for the rich and famous, but nothing could be further from the truth. Even if your assets are modest, *and especially if you have children*, having a will is a must. It's less costly than you might think to ensure your last wishes are known and carried out. If you happen to die without a will or estate plan, the court will decide for you who receives your assets and who will care for your children.

I caution you against trying to do it yourself with an online legal website. Yes, you can get a "cheap will" and it's better than nothing; however it may be deemed worthless by a judge if it doesn't abide by the letter of the law in your state. Paying a good estate planning attorney a few hundred dollars to do this right for your family the first time will save stress and heartache during an already difficult time. Ask friends and family for a referral and interview at least two attorneys before selecting one to handle your estate plan. This person will work in tandem with your insurance agent and tax professional to ensure a good solid estate plan.

~

What do we loathe paying more than insurance premiums? Taxes! I don't want you to pay any more in taxes than you're legally required to, which is why you need a super nerdy CPA or tax professional. The US tax code is extraordinarily complex and I don't see it changing any time soon. I've been an accountant for almost two decades, and I don't even do my own taxes! I got a "D" in my Tax Accounting class in college despite being on the honor roll, so I'm smart enough to know when I need help. A tax professional's full time job is to stay on top of the changing regulations and ensure his or her clients aren't paying any more in tax payments than required. I know my CPA saves me more money than I pay him to do my annual tax returns. If you're a small business owner or have some level of complexity with your tax returns, I highly recommend you hire a tax professional to help you.

Although we don't particularly like discussing insurance, estate planning, or taxes, these all have an impact on our family's bottom line. Having a smart insurance agent, tax professional, and attorney on your money team is a must. The good ones will save you more money with their advice than they cost you.

ACTION ITEMS

Do you know what type of insurances you own and the coverages you have? What insurance gaps do you have that need to be filled? Do you have a will and/or estate plan? If so, when was the last time it was updated to reflect your family's current situation? Do you have a tax professional to help you with your returns? Make an appointment to meet with your insurance agent, attorney, or CPA to take care of any loose ends.

CHAPTER 45

Who's on Your Money Team?

"**P**lans go wrong for lack of advice; many advisors bring success," said King Solomon, who is considered to be one of the wisest men to ever walk the face of the earth. If he thought it was a good idea to have advisors, maybe *we* ought to pay attention. Who is on your Money Team? We have this idea that only millionaires or billionaires need a Money Team, but we all need one if we want to achieve financial freedom.

Even if you are a numbers person, like me, it's still difficult to be an expert in every area of money. I'm proficient at saving and managing money, but I need the input of qualified experts when it comes to taxes, insurance, and investments. Some of these fields—like tax accounting—are a labyrinth of rules and regulations. You'd be foolish and reckless to try and go it alone. When selecting people for a spot on your Money Team, ensure they "have the heart of a teacher, not the heart of a salesman," as financial guru, Dave Ramsey says. These financial professionals should explain things in a way you can understand and they should welcome your questions. Who should be on your Money Team? Here are candidates to consider.

Your spouse (or other responsible friend or family member if you're single) should be on your Money Team. This person knows your weaknesses and strengths and will be able to give you honest feedback and help you uncover your blind spots. If you are married, it's imperative you discuss major purchases and changes to your insurance or investments with them first.

A CPA, Accountant, or other Tax Professional will ensure you are compliant with current tax laws without paying more than necessary. As your financial life becomes fuller and more complex, a good tax professional will help you minimize your tax burden so you can protect your nest egg. My CPA is a vital part of my Money Team because keeping up with tax law changes is a full time job.

We've already discussed the importance of estate planning as a part of your Financial Roadmap, which is just one of the reasons why you need an **attorney** on your Money Team. Consult with an attorney before entering into business deals, partnerships, leasing agreements, and other contracts. Legal documents are confusing, and if you sign something you don't understand, it could cost you dearly in the long run. Attorneys can also be invaluable resources for adoption, custody issues, and divorce.

Most of us hate paying our insurance premiums every month, but these policies protect us against catastrophic financial blows. **Your insurance agent** should help you navigate the various choices for coverage to ensure your risks are covered. It's wise to talk with several insurance agents, gathering information, and comparing prices so you can make an educated decision on your insurance needs.

If you already have some retirement assets, then you definitely need the expertise of a **financial advisor or investment professional**. The world of investing is confusing and there are tens of thousands of different investments and mutual funds from which to choose. A financial advisor will assist you in determining what types of investments and in what proportions your retirement funds should be allocated. Be warned that not all investment professionals have your best interests at heart. Because investing can be complicated, it's not hard for us to get confused and be embarrassed to ask questions. However, if we don't ask good questions and get them answered to our satisfaction, it can cost us serious money over our investing lifetime. I strongly encourage you interview at least two advisors before making your decision.

Depending on your personal situation, there may be additional players to consider adding to your Money Team. If you are struggling with your budget and debt reduction plan, you may want to enlist the help of a **financial coach**. If you plan on buying a house within the next year or so, connect with a **mortgage broker** or the residential lending officer at your bank. They will help you get your financial ducks in a row so the mortgage process goes smoothly when you're ready to buy. I would also interview two or more **Realtors®** several months before putting your house on the market. This is one of the biggest financial transactions you may make in your lifetime and you want a professional real estate agent to handle it, not your Uncle Joe who recently just passed the test for his real estate license! If you have kids in middle or high school, connecting with a **college planning expert** is an excellent idea.

In general, be cautious of having close friends of family members as part of your Money Team. I've seen my clients make bad decisions regarding insurance policies and investments, because they were sold to them by their best friend or father-in-law. If you are considering this, be sure to get a second or third opinion before bringing this person onto your Money Team. Keep in mind you don't have to formally ask these folks, "Will you please be on my Money Team?"

Some people try to find "expert" advice on the cheap. The cost of hiring an amateur to be on your Money Team can be very expensive indeed. However, I don't want you to overpay for expert advice either. I do recommend you get a second opinion on your insurance, investments, etc. every few years to make sure you're still receiving solid advice and a fair price. Be certain to meet with the members of your Money Team on a regular basis to ensure you are on track with the various parts of your Financial Roadmap and value their contribution.

ACTION ITEMS

Ask yourself these questions: "Who is currently on my Money Team? Am I happy with their performance and level of advice?

Who is missing from my Money Team? Am I sitting down with the members of my Money Team at least annually?" Based on your answers to these questions, fill the gaps on your Money Team.

CHAPTER 46

Don't Take My Word for It

It's fabulous to have a team of competent financial experts assisting you with the complex world of investing, insurance, mortgages, and the like. However, this doesn't let you off the hook for learning more about these money topics. *You* are ultimately responsible for your financial health so you need to do your homework. Just as it's wise to get a second opinion on a serious medical diagnosis, it's also a good idea to do the same with major money decisions.

Problems can arise when you never (or rarely) question the advice of someone on your Money Team. I want you to *know enough to be dangerous* when it comes to investing, insurance, mortgages, and wills. I want you to ask questions about the advice you are receiving because it means you are paying attention and you're learning new things. You should never be afraid to question or challenge the experts on your Money Team. You are the boss and they work for you!

If someone on your Money Team says, "Take my word for it: you need this investment/insurance policy…" I say, *don't take their word for it*! Do some research by reading or listening to a book on the subject. Ask other professionals who you respect in the same field for their take on the matter. If your insurance agent or investment advisor gets mad or offended because you are questioning their advice, it's time to move on to someone else. A solid professional will welcome your questions and encourage you to expand your understanding of the financial products you own.

There are times when my coaching clients question my recommendations, and I welcome it. I know I'm not perfect and I certainly don't have all of the answers. I encourage my clients to learn more about money management and take ownership of their own financial health.

Most of us dislike confrontation, but the time may come when you have to "fire" someone from your Money Team. We've all worked for companies who have that one employee who's long overdue to get the boot. *"Why is he even allowed to still be working here?"* we wonder. It puts a strain on company morale when the "bad apple" isn't fired sooner rather than later. This same tension can permeate our financial lives when someone on our Money Team needs to go. Maybe your insurance agent isn't giving you good customer service, or your CPA "forgot" to tell you to pay your estimated tax payments last year and now you have penalties due to the IRS. Sitting and seething about their financial transgressions will only make you miserable. It's time to take action!

The first and hardest step is to confront the under-performing person on your Money Team and clear the air. Tell them exactly what the problem is and why you feel wronged. Give them the chance to explain their side. It's up to you whether you want to give them the chance to rectify the mistake or not. If you choose to give the person a second chance and keep them on your Money Team, at least put them on "probation." Tell them exactly what you expect to change and the timeframe.

CASE STUDY: "INVESTING WITH A FRIEND"

Carl, a manager at a local credit union, knew his financial advisor, Mark, from Habitat for Humanity, a charity that builds homes for the poor. Having recently accepted the position at the credit union, Carl had a sizable 401(k) from his previous employer which needed to be rolled over into an IRA so it could be actively managed. He felt like Mark was a good solid guy and a smart investor who deserved a place on his Money Team.

Three years after his rollover was transferred to Mark's care, Carl read a thought-provoking book about investing which warned of the hidden fees in many mutual funds. Carl decided to do some investigating on his own and researched the investments in his IRA to see how they stacked up. He felt confident his buddy Mark had surely put his money in low-cost funds with above average track records.

To Carl's dismay, he realized that over half of the funds Mark had selected were dismal performers. Many of these underperforming funds were also charging higher than average fees. Carl felt betrayed by his friend whom he had trusted to look out for his family's best interests. He also was mad at himself for not discovering these facts sooner. Working for a credit union, Carl chastised himself for not being more financially savvy.

Carl called and made an appointment with an independent financial planner, Dana, who came highly recommended by his colleagues at work. Dana reviewed Carl's investments and confirmed his suspicions. He was paying too many fees for underperforming funds in his IRA, which would have a significant impact on his balance at retirement if not rectified.

Carl seethed for a week over his discovery but knew he had to call Mark and confront him. He wasn't just going to transfer his IRA over to Dana's direction without at least giving his friend an explanation. Carl had some trepidation over what Mark's reaction would be. Would he plead for a second chance? Would the next building project with Habitat for Humanity be awkward if Carl was no longer Mark's investment client? Although he didn't know the answers before picking up the phone, Carl knew he was ultimately responsible for the financial wellbeing of his family. He wasn't willing to allow someone else's feelings to sway his decision to take care of his future.

ACTION ITEMS

Have you ever had to fire someone on your Money Team? Is there someone on your Money Team who is overdue to be let go? What areas of personal finance do you need to learn more about in order to know enough to be dangerous and hold your Money Team accountable?

PART FIVE

Love & Money

CHAPTER 47

Money and Relationships

Both relationships and money are woven into the daily fabric of our lives. At their best, our relationships can be warm, supportive, and fulfilling; at their worst they can be contentious, drama-filled, and even destructive. Toss money into the mix and it's easy to see how it can be like throwing gasoline on a fire.

Money has the potential to be a source of contention in relationships, but it doesn't *have* to be. Many relationships crumble because of money issues, and it's usually due to a lack of communication. Here's the good news: couples who regularly discuss their finances with each other—and have a plan—almost always have strong marriages. In the chapters to come, I'll talk about ways to take off the boxing gloves and get on the same page with your significant other when it comes to personal finance.

Money problems aren't just a factor in our romantic relationships. I've seen money issues come between friends, siblings, parents and their children. It's vital to be aware of the emotional landmines surrounding relationships because there's so much at stake. A misstep in one of these areas could cost you more than money. It's pretty simple to earn more money to fix a financial mistake, but sometimes relationships are broken beyond repair.

The good news is this section is *not* titled "Love *or* Money," but "Love *and* Money." You don't have to choose between the two! Achieving both healthy finances and fulfilling relationships is totally doable. A word of caution before we delve into the topic of love and money: if your spouse, partner, boyfriend or girlfriend is attempting to control you with money—there is a problem. If your spouse, partner, boyfriend or girlfriend is attempting to persuade you to spend your money unwisely or go into debt against your better judgment—there is a problem! In these instances, money is a symptom of a deeper psychological issue. There's no shame in seeking the help of a good counselor or psychologist to assist you in working through those issues.

When I left Jeff, I was smart enough to realize that spending seven years in a co-dependent relationship had warped my views on both love and money. My company offered a confidential counseling service to any employee and I took advantage of it. I knew if I didn't uncover those faulty mindsets regarding love and money, I would be doomed to repeat my mistakes with the next relationship. My counselor, Dave, gave me the perfect blend of compassion and truth I needed to create healthy boundaries that would serve me well into the future. If you feel like you are really struggling with an emotional money issue, do yourself a favor and seek the help you need. Your company's benefit plan may even cover your counseling costs, as mine did.

ACTION ITEMS

Do feel like you must choose between love and money in your relationships? Are you open to receiving counseling on an issue with which you may be struggling?

CHAPTER 48

Get Financially Naked

I'm amazed at how many couples have no qualms about getting physically naked with each other before getting married, but keep their financial details tightly under wraps. With money issues being cited as the first or second cause of almost 75% of divorces, this is a conversation that has to take place.

Don't wait until you're engaged or moving in together to start having money conversations with your boyfriend or girlfriend! When you first start dating someone, just observe how they talk about and handle money. Do they allude to the fact they have a ton of bills, credit card debt, or big student loan payments? Do they always insist on paying for dates, or insist on you paying? Or are they "even-steven" when it comes to going out? Do they admire financially successful individuals or refer to them as "greedy rich people"? These observations will give you clues as to how they handle and think about money.

When you begin to get more serious with your significant other, now's the time to start having more in-depth conversations as money topics come up. You don't necessarily have to set up a formal meeting and say, *"Now we're going to have a serious talk about money!"* Remember, just because your significant other does something differently from you with their money, it doesn't necessarily mean it's wrong. Our past

185

experiences and what our parents taught us, or didn't teach us, about money can influence our behavior today.

~

Once you are officially engaged, I highly recommend you take a personal finance class together. Some churches will have a money component to their premarital program. At the very least, read or listen to a book on money management together. Going through this material as a couple will spur in-depth conversations between you and your fiancé regarding personal finance. It may also be helpful to have a coaching session with a financial counselor or money coach to help you navigate the combining of your finances. This is especially true if one of you has been married previously, there are step children involved, or one of you is coming into the relationship with a disproportionate amount of either debt or assets.

Before you get married is the time to get completely financially naked with your significant other. No hidden purchases, debt, or savings. Talk about how you are going to handle the day-to-day financial transactions in your house. Who is going to be responsible for making bill payments, buying groceries, purchasing items for the house? Is all of your money going to be in one joint account, or will you keep some spending money separate?

If you have these conversations prior to getting married and work out the issues, you'll be much more likely to have a strong, loving marriage that lasts. However, you may discover there are deal breaker issues. Isn't it better you find this out now rather than *after* the wedding?

~

Already married? We like to tease about hiding our purchases from our husbands or wives so we don't "get in trouble;" however keeping money secrets from your spouse is no joke. We all need to prioritize honest communication about money. It doesn't matter if you are hiding purchases, credit cards, or even savings accounts from your significant other, "financial infidelity" can wreak havoc on a relationship.

The first thing to ask is this: "*Why* do I feel the need to hide this from my spouse?" Maybe you know you shouldn't be buying more clothes, toys for the kids, electronics, etc. on the credit card. Maybe you're squirrelling away money in a separate savings account because you're afraid your husband or wife will find a way to spend it. When you dig down to the real reason for the financial infidelity, you'll find *the issue usually isn't money; it's trust.* You need to talk to your partner and get these concerns out in the open. If you've tried this in the past and had a disastrous outcome, enlist the help of a marriage counselor or financial therapist, if necessary.

I recently counseled a couple who had been married for six months, yet hadn't combined their money. They were in their early 30's and had both been used to handling their money independently. They loved and trusted each other; however, their methods for managing and spending money were a little different. I was able to help them blend their styles together and formulate a plan that honored their differences, yet unified their finances.

If you do communicate regularly with your spouse or partner about money, you'll increase the odds of having a rock solid relationship. Communicate early and often! This is just one of many reasons why I highly recommend meeting at least once a month to discuss the household budget and other money matters. And if you are engaged or seriously dating someone, it's important to get "financially naked" with each other before walking down the aisle.

If you're nervous about doing this, pick up a copy of *Get Financially Naked: How to Talk Money with your Honey* by Manisha Thakor and Sharon Kedar. It is packed with tips and scripts for making money talks with your honey more pleasant and productive!

ACTION ITEMS

If you are dating or engaged, how much do you know about your significant other's financial beliefs and behaviors? How much do they know about your money situation? If you're married, are you keeping money secrets from your spouse? If so, why? Schedule a time to sit down with your partner and get "financially naked" if you haven't already done so.

CHAPTER 49

His Money, Her Money, Our Money

arried couples with separate checking or savings accounts may certainly conjure up images of financial infidelity between husbands and wives. Having all of your money in a joint account necessitates frequent communication about financial matters, which is a plus. However, I think there are certain situations when separate accounts can be a good idea. First, let me put forth a few disclaimers. I think deliberately hiding money or debt from your spouse or partner is a horrible idea. *Separate money does not mean secret money!* I also firmly believe spouses should have access to all accounts, even if they don't normally exercise that access. The reason a couple might want to separate *some* of their money is to reduce, not increase, disagreements over spending.

If you're not married yet, having separate accounts is definitely okay. In fact, I don't think you should add your fiancé to your checking and savings accounts until you are legally married. Engagements are occasionally cancelled and it can be an enormous pain to have your ex-girlfriend/boyfriend/fiancé removed from your accounts.

Having separate accounts for your discretionary spending money can foster a sense of responsibility and freedom. In a marriage relationship, there is usually one person who is more naturally inclined to handle the majority of the financial transactions for the household (paying bills, balancing the checking accounts, and making transfers to savings or investment accounts.) There's certainly nothing wrong with this, as long as the couple is having *regular* conversations (at least monthly) about the family finances. If the less financially involved spouse has at least one account they're wholly responsible for, it ensures they are engaged and educated about the basics of money management. The other bonus to having your fun money in your own account is you have the control to spend the money as you please *without* owing an explanation to your husband or wife. Just be sure to decide as a couple in advance how much money will go to each spouse's discretionary spending account every month.

This idea works really well for me and my husband. We have three checking accounts: our household bill account, my checking account, and his checking account. The bank automatically transfers money from our personal checking accounts to the household bill account every two weeks. We pay the mortgage, utilities, insurance, groceries, and general household expenses from this account. From our separate checking accounts, we each pay for our own gas, entertainment, clothing, and other fun stuff. This way, Nick doesn't complain that I'm spending "too much" on shoes, purses, or jewelry. And I don't complain when he spends his fun money on the latest electronics. I know other couples who do this, but rather than using checking accounts, they put their fun money on prepaid Visa cards.

When you're part of a blended family, having some money in separate accounts can be very beneficial. A great deal of turmoil and disagreements can erupt between spouses when step children (and even grandchildren) are in the picture. Not only do parenting styles differ, but also spending choices. Sometimes it helps for husbands and wives to agree on a total amount to spend on "her kids" and "his kids," and then each parent decide individually how to allocate the total among their own kids and the various categories. If you've already agreed to the total amount and are sticking to it, then there's no reason to bicker over the details! (As a side note, if you are getting married for the second or third time and there are step children involved, please consult an attorney for the proper estate planning.)

Occasionally, one spouse knows they have a tendency to overspend and fully agrees that he/she *shouldn't* have free rein over all of the accounts. Some spenders feel like they can't fully trust themselves to behave with the debit card or checking account, and would prefer to have a certain amount of cash every week or a pre-paid Visa card with a set amount of money on it. If you're a chronic over-drafter, it may be a good solution. This only works when the overspending spouse *admits and agrees* to this. If you are trying to control your spouse by imposing an allowance on them without their consent, it will likely end with a trip to divorce court. The end goal is to slowly build up this spouse's financial self-control muscles and eventually become an equal partner in the household money management.

I do think married couples should keep the majority of their money in joint accounts. If you're married and are still keeping all of your money separate, it might be a sign of trust issues which should be talked over with a counselor or therapist. Deliberately hiding credit cards or even savings accounts from your husband or wife is a terrible idea. I also firmly believe spouses should have access to all accounts. Remember, the reason a couple may want to separate some of their money is to *reduce* disagreements over spending.

ACTION ITEM

Do you and your spouse keep all of your money together or do you keep some of it separate? Why?

CHAPTER 50

Engaging the Uninvolved Spouse

What do you do when your spouse or partner doesn't want to be involved in the financial decision making process? The "Uninvolved Spouse" problem isn't uncommon in families, but it's a serious one. If you're both not openly communicating about and participating in the family finances, it's a recipe for conflict.

SCENARIO #1: THE "CLUELESS ONE"

Jamie is an investment advisor and her husband, Matt, is a freelance writer who works from home and takes care of their toddler, Isabella. Jamie handles all of the bill paying, investing, and other major financial decision making. Matt knows his wife is a money expert and he trusts her to handle the family finances. You might be thinking this is a good arrangement for Matt and Jamie.

However, Matt doesn't have a clue about good financial management. His parents never talked about money—probably because they never had any. When Jamie tries to talk to him about major financial issues, his eyes glaze over and he mentally

192

checks out. The entire burden of managing the household money is on Jamie and she is feeling stressed out because of it.

But what happens if Jamie and Matt get divorced? Or what if—God forbid—Jamie is killed in a freak car accident? Will Matt even know which banks and brokerages are housing their accounts and how to access the money?

Situations like this happen all the time. I've had numerous tearful widows and distraught divorcees show up for coaching appointments, clutching a box or thick file full of bills and bank statements, needing assistance with sorting out the financial details. It's hard enough to deal with the pain of a divorce or death without financial confusion thrown on top of it.

Here are some tips to get the "clueless one" educated and informed on the very important topic of their own finances.

- First and foremost, do *not* patronize your spouse or make them feel bad for lacking money management skills. It's likely they are already embarrassed or ashamed of their lack of financial knowledge. If you add to this feeling, your partner will shut down and withdraw rather than engage.
- Let's get the Matts of the world a sound understanding of the financial basics. There are plenty of great books, audio programs, and videos out there to learn the basics of money management. Couples can read or watch them together and discuss the concepts and how they apply to their situation. My blog is chock full of articles, videos, and podcast on the basics of personal finance: http://christineluken.com/blog
- Matt and Jamie need to hold a monthly budget meeting to discuss the state of their finances. These meetings might only be five or ten minutes long, but they will go a long way in keeping both people engaged and up to speed.
- Jamie needs to set up a folder or file box with all of the important financial information for Matt to access should something happen to her. This file should contain bank

account numbers and access instructions, plus contact information for bankers, investment brokers, and insurance agents. There should also be a copy of their will or trust and attorney contact info.

- By following these steps, "The Clueless One" can be transformed over time into the spouse who is educated, engaged, and involved with the family finances. This will help the couple walk in unity and reduce conflict and resentment.

~

What if your spouse isn't clueless, but rather is like a spoiled child when it comes to money? Honestly, this scenario is worse than the first one. When there is a parent/child dynamic between spouses, it creates an imbalance in the marriage relationship which will cause friction and fighting between husband and wife. Let's take a look at how this scenario might play out.

SCENARIO #2: THE SPOILED CHILD

Meet Jenna and Rick. They have five-year-old twin girls, Aria and Anna. Rick is the Vice President of Operations for a major manufacturing corporation, while Jenna is a volunteer at the girls' school. Rick makes a great salary and handles most of the bill paying, but not by choice. He feels as though he cannot trust Jenna to take care of the bills, because in the past she had a habit of racking up late fees and overdrafts.

Jenna is an only child and, growing up, her wealthy father and mother rarely said "no" to their "little princess". Unfortunately, Jenna's parents did not teach her the value of a dollar or proper money management, as Rick's hard-working middle class parents did. For example, Jenna was given a brand new car for her sixteenth birthday, completely paid for and fully insured by her parents. Rick's parents sold him his mom's old car, at a discount, once he proved to be a responsible driver, several months after he was legally able to drive.

Rick feels like he has three little girls to take care of, not two. He does make good money, but he's not wealthy like his father-in-law. Rick doesn't disclose the amount of money he's putting into his 401(k) or savings account to Jenna, because he knows she'll want to spend it on another vacation, granite counter tops, or something else to "keep up with the Joneses." Rick wants a wife who is a partner in the family finances, not a spoiled child whose messes he is constantly cleaning up.

Wow, this type of situation is really tough. I know it from personal experience. Years ago when I was engaged to Jeff, he exhibited many of these "Spoiled Child" behaviors, despite coming from a working class family. I remember feeling angry and resentful that I had to be the responsible one. I felt like Jeff was more like my teenage son than a true partner, which is why I'm no longer with him. So, what's the solution?

First and foremost, I would recommend both financial coaching and marriage counseling to a couple in this scenario. The "responsible" partner, in this case Rick, is probably harboring some anger and resentment toward his wife and it needs to be dealt with in a constructive manner. Jenna, the "spoiled child" needs a financial coach and marriage counselor to help her see the error of her ways in a non-judgmental environment. It's likely that Jenna will be much more receptive to feedback and education from a third party, rather than from her husband. In this way, she can learn the baby steps necessary to become a full partner in the family finances.

Just as you wouldn't hand over the keys of your new BMW to an inexperienced teenage driver, we don't want to set up the family finances for disaster by having the recovering "spoiled child" take on too much responsibility too soon. Here's how I would counsel a couple like Rick and Jenna. I'd suggest Rick turn over responsibility for one area of the budget to Jenna, such as groceries. If Jenna admits she probably can't be trusted with a debit card yet, Rick would need to give her cash or a pre-paid Visa card for purchasing the family's groceries for the month. This will provide a microcosm environment for practicing the budgeting skills she's learning from her financial coach.

Jenna will need to track her purchases, pay attention to what she's spending, and ensure she has enough to last her the entire month. Rick is also going to have to prepare himself to say "no" if Jenna asks for more grocery money before the end of the month. It's important for recovering "spoiled children" to learn there is a finite amount of money and *when it's gone, it's gone.* Rick has to be okay with eating hot dogs and macaroni and cheese for the last week of the month if that's what it takes to drive this important lesson home. As Jenna realizes it's much more satisfying to be a responsible financial partner with Rick, they can move to a more balanced division of handling the family finances.

The parent/child financial dynamic is not an easy one to overcome, but it can be accomplished if both spouses admit their shortfalls and enlist the help of a good financial coach, marriage counselor, and/or financial therapist.

And I would hope this goes without saying, but if your husband or wife is either a "clueless one" or a "spoiled child," you should *never* refer to them that way out loud!

ACTION ITEMS

If your spouse is currently uninvolved in the family finances, is he or she more like the "clueless one" or the "spoiled child?" What steps will you take in the upcoming weeks to get them educated and positively involved in family money matters? What outside resources can you draw on to help you in the process? Are you the "clueless one" or the "spoiled child?" Are you willing to embrace change and become a responsible partner in the family finances?

CHAPTER 51

Are You a Financial Enabler?

As you might have guessed, I used to be a big-time financial enabler. Jeff had terrible money habits. He spent every penny he made (and then some) and he changed jobs the way some people change their socks. I was young and in love, and I thought with enough support and encouragement, I could help Jeff become all that I thought he could be. Over the course of the seven-year relationship, I cleaned up countless financial messes for my fiancé. Unfortunately, the more I "helped" Jeff, the worse things became.

You see, my help wasn't really helping him personally or financially. I was shielding Jeff from the negative consequences of his financial misbehavior, so he never learned his lesson. I became bitter and resentful over always having to clean up his messes. *But it wasn't his fault, it was mine.*

As a Financial Lifeguard, I see this situation come up during my coaching sessions with couples. Many times they are "helping" their irresponsible adult children and constantly bailing them out of their financial disasters. Throw grandchildren into the mix, and the grandparents feel guilty for not helping. It's definitely a sensitive subject that can cause a good deal of drama and conflict for a family. Fortunately, because of my personal experience, I'm able to assist people in breaking the vicious cycle of *financial enabling*.

Here are Some Signs You Are Enabling, Not Helping:

- The person expects you to help and uses guilt to try to manipulate you.
- The person makes the same kinds of financial mistakes over and over.
- The person seems to get worse, not better, after you help them.
- You are suffering financially as a result of helping the other person.
- The situation is a constant source of stress—and you feel bitter and resentful.

The first and hardest step in breaking this cycle is admitting you are a financial enabler and *you* are part of the problem. You have been shielding your loved one from the financial consequences of their own behavior, which isn't a good thing for either of you. Once you have reached this conclusion, you need to arrange a sit-down meeting to discuss the situation. Be prepared for the other person to be upset and even to say that you are unloving or uncaring for allowing them face their own consequences. Depending on the situation, you may need to set up a timeline for change. The person will likely test you, so make sure you are mentally prepared to stick to your guns.

Case Study: The Overly Generous Friend

A relative of mine, Claire, formed a friendship with her coworker, Jane, who was 17 years her junior. Claire's children were grown and out of the house, so she enjoyed her time with Jane and Jane's young son, Simon. They would go out to lunch or the movies a few times a month. In the beginning, Claire would occasionally surprise Jane by paying the lunch tab or buying the movie tickets for all of them. As time went on, though, Claire noticed that Jane would seem to "forget" to go to the ATM before their outings. One day Claire, Jane, and Simon were at the movie theater to watch the latest Disney flick. As they stood in line for refreshments, Jane excused herself to go to the restroom. "Get me a large popcorn and a Diet Coke and whatever Simon wants," she called over her shoulder as she walked off. Claire was seething inside because this was not the first time this had happened, and she knew Jane wouldn't be paying her back for these movie snacks. Claire swallowed her anger as she approached the snack counter, smiling at Simon and asking, "What kind of candy do want, honey?"

What should Claire do? First, Claire needs to realize she is a financial enabler. By not confronting Jane and letting her mooching go unchecked, Claire can only expect the behavior to continue. It's best that Claire waits until her anger has subsided to have this conversation—in person—with Jane. The conversation might start like this: "Jane, you know I love spending time with you and Simon, and I consider you to be like extended family to me. When we go out to the movies or lunch, I do enjoy occasionally treating you and Simon, but lately it seems like you're assuming I'm always going to pay. Unfortunately, my budget for entertainment is limited and I can't pay your way every time we go out…"

Now, please understand I'm *not* saying you should never help your loved ones when they are having a hard time or just because you're feeling generous. The above guidelines are for the repeat offender who is always in financial trouble and seems to get worse—not better—when you "help" them. If you have a friend or relative who's normally a very responsible person come to you because of an unforeseen situation, such as a job loss or divorce, by all means help them! But only assist them if you can afford to give them the money. If they happen to pay you back later when they get back on their feet, great. If not, don't be offended by it. *If you think you'll be mad if they never pay you back the money, then don't give it to them.* Period. Many relationships have been ruined because of this very situation.

ACTION ITEMS

Are you—or have you been—a financial enabler? What steps do you need to take in order to restore balance to the situation? It's possible that personal counseling may also be needed to work out these issues in a family or relationship. I also highly recommend reading the book *Boundaries: When to Say Yes, How to Say No to Take Control of Your Life* by Dr. Henry Cloud & Dr. John Townsend.

CHAPTER 52

The Perils of Cosigning a Loan

It's never a good idea to cosign a loan for a friend or family member, whether it's a credit card, car loan, or a mortgage. Cosigning is hazardous to your financial and relational health. There are both money consequences and relationship consequences when someone defaults on a loan on which you've cosigned. Potential risks include seizure of bank accounts, garnishment of your paycheck, a black eye to your credit report, and ruined relationships!

By now, you know I have made an abundance of financial mistakes in my past. Surprisingly, this isn't one of them! However, I've encountered more than a few people who have reaped the negative consequences of cosigning a loan for a friend or family member.

I think it's important to understand *why* a bank would want a cosigner for a loan in the first place. Banks typically require a cosigner on a loan when the applicant doesn't meet their lending criteria. This usually means the applicant—your friend or family member—has bad credit, no credit, too much debt, not enough income, or some combination of those things. Banks have lending formulas down to a science. Lending is their business and they have determined that your friend or family member is a bad business risk.

What does it mean to cosign a debt? Essentially, you are volunteering to be *legally and financially responsible for the entire debt* if the original borrower does not pay for any reason. If the person becomes unable to pay because of financial hardship or negligence, the lender will come knocking on your door expecting you to *pay in full*. If you try to avoid paying it, the lender can submit negative information on your credit report and take legal steps to recover the money including wage garnishment and seizing bank accounts. Cosigning removes the financial and legal consequences of the debt from the other person and places them squarely on your own shoulders.

"But I want to help!" you might say. Then give them the money they need. If you can't afford to give them the money, then you can't afford to cosign. *Default rates on cosigned loans are as high as 75%.* Yes, you heard me right! If your friend or family member is truly worthy of the help they need, see if you can get a group of people together to help pitch in. You could even set up a GoFundMe account or use a similar venue to raise the money.

"My brother/girlfriend/best friend will be upset with me, is pressuring me, or is making me feel guilty about saying NO." I understand that money is emotional! However, it's important to realize when you make financial decisions out of emotion, it's usually going to be an expensive learning experience and one you will likely regret.

"What about cosigning for my spouse, fiancé, boyfriend, or girlfriend?" If you are married, this is a non-issue. When your minister says, "And the two have become one," it means financially, too. Do *not* cosign for your fiancé, boyfriend, or girlfriend. Some weddings never happen! It's bad enough to experience a breakup without being stuck with a monthly payment as a reminder of the person you want to forget. This happened to a friend of mine in college who cosigned a car loan for her then-boyfriend. Within a few months, he wrecked the car, they broke up, and the lender came after my friend for payment. Trust me, it wasn't pretty!

"Should I cosign a car loan for one of my children, since they don't have any credit?" I would much prefer you teach

them how to save up and pay cash for a car. They will take much better care of a car when they have some skin in the game. A secured credit card is a better method to build credit than to indoctrinate your kids into a lifetime habit of car payments.

Cosigning when you can't afford to foot the bill is putting your own financial heath at risk. Your income is the life blood of your personal finances. If you suddenly have a large payment to make on someone else's debt, you're going to lack funds for your own goals. It's like pledging to donate more blood to the Red Cross than you have to give. Imagine that you decide to donate blood once a month. The average human body contains ten pints of blood; usually one pint is taken during blood donation. What if your friend pledged to donate one pint of blood for three months, and asked you to cosign. If he didn't donate the blood, the Red Cross could come for you at any time and demand you "pay up" the balance all at once. The human body can't afford to lose more than three or four pints at one time without risking major problems. I don't think any of us in our right minds would ever agree to do this. And yet, people do the equivalent with their money when they cosign!

I hope I have thoroughly convinced you of the evils of cosigning, and I implore you to avoid it like the plague! Proverbs 22:26–27 (New Living Translation) says: "Don't agree to guarantee another person's debt or put up security for someone else. If you can't pay it, even your bed will be snatched from under you." See, even God thinks it's a bad idea!

ACTION ITEM

Have you or a friend or family member ever cosigned a loan for someone else? What was the end result?

Chapter 53

What's a Few Bucks Between Friends

"	If you lend your brother-in-law $100 and you never see him again, was it worth it?" ~ Old Joke
	Have you ever loaned a friend or coworker $20, $50, or more? Did you notice things between you felt a little strained until the debt was repaid? It wasn't your imagination. When you loan money to someone, friend or family member, it changes the emotional fabric of the relationship. King Solomon said, "The borrower is slave to the lender." This is similar to the law of gravity in that it doesn't matter if you *want* it to be true or not, it always is. You may say, "Lending my brother money isn't going to change our relationship." Yes, indeed, it will; whether you want it to or not.

CASE STUDY: THE CHRISTMAS PRESENT LOAN

Christa's friend and coworker, Tamara, came to her distraught in mid-December asking for a loan. "My ex-husband didn't make his child support payment and I have no money to buy the boys their Christmas presents! Can I borrow $825 and I'll pay you back as soon as the child support comes in? He said I'll have it by the end of the month." Christa certainly had enough money in her savings to help her friend and she didn't want Tamara's sweet boys, who were 5 and 8 years old, to have no Santa Claus this year, so she lent her the money.

Come mid-January, Tamara claimed she still didn't have her December child support payment. Christa noticed her friend seemed evasive and they weren't talking or hanging out as much as usual. Christa would find herself judging Tamara's actions. "If she can afford to go out to lunch today, she can surely afford to start paying me back some of that $825," Christa would think to herself. "Maybe she lied to me about the child support payment. Her ex-husband has always paid on time in the past…"

In February, Tamara took a job with another company. Christa seethed at the fact her calls went unanswered and she finally wrote off the money as gone forever. Over a decade later, Christa feels a lingering resentment when she remembers exactly how much money Tamara still owes her.

Most of us want to help our friends and family when a need arises, financial or otherwise, and that's a good thing. However, extreme caution must be used in the area of lending money. In fact, I think if you do lend money to a friend, you should go into it thinking that the money is a gift, not a loan. *If you can't afford to give your friend the money, then you can't afford to lend it to them.* Not only will you risk the relationship, but you're risking your own financial wellbeing.

You also can't afford the emotional and relational consequences of the loan potentially going bad. I think most of us have experienced this situation at least once. If you cherish your relationship with this person, you either need to explain to them with love that you cannot risk your own financial health to help them, or give them the money. (We're assuming here this person isn't financially irresponsible.) This isn't just stressful for the person making the loan; it's also an emotional burden on the person borrowing the money.

CASE STUDY: THE BUSINESS OPPORTUNITY "LOAN"

My friend had an excellent business opportunity come his way which had the potential to gain worldwide exposure for his ideas and drastically increase his income. He came to me and asked to borrow the money via a structured note. I honestly didn't feel comfortable lending the full amount he needed, but said I would be willing to "invest" $2,500 in his business opportunity for a 10% upside. I was fully prepared to lose the entire $2,500 if the deal went south. I went into it thinking it was a gift or an investment of which I could potentially lose 100%, but I was willing to risk it.

Unfortunately, the other party in the deal with my friend didn't live up to the hype and the whole opportunity, along with the money, evaporated. My friend called me, apologized for losing my investment, and said he was taking legal action against the offending party in an effort to reclaim the money for me and the other investors. I told him not to worry about it, as I was already mentally prepared for this worst case scenario.

Several months later, I had this nagging feeling I needed to call this friend and reiterate that the failed investment was not his fault and the debt was completely forgiven on my part. I honestly argued with myself, "But I already told him! He's going to think it's weird that I'm calling to tell him again, because he's probably forgotten about it and moved on." So I called him and said, "Hey man, I want you to know this loan is forgiven. I'm shredding the promissory note and I want you to do the same." His relief was palpable. "Thank you! I can't tell you how much this has been weighing on my mind," my friend said. I replied, "Our friendship is worth more than this $2,500 business investment, so let's wipe the slate clean. I knew there was the possibility of losing the money from the start, and I was fully prepared for it going in. No hard feelings, my friend."

There have been times when I have loaned much smaller amounts of money, fully expecting it to be repaid, and lost the relationship because the other person never paid me back. However, when I treat the loan as a gift, I'm actually surprised and delighted if the person repays. And I must say it's very rare I lend people money these days. However, I am quite generous with my friends, family, and charitable organizations.

Think about this when you are asking to borrow money from a friend or family member. You'll likely feel burdened around them until you pay them back the money. This can definitely make family gatherings around the holidays uncomfortable when you owe money to your parent or sibling.

ACTION ITEMS

Have you had a loan to a friend or family member go bad? Were you the borrower or the lender? How was the relationship affected?

CHAPTER 54

Parents, Teach Your Children to Swim

arents, if you've ever had a drowning scare with your child, you know how frightful it can be. Once you pull your child to safety and calm him or her down, your first call is to schedule swimming lessons. Why? You want to make sure it will never happen again. What if you hadn't been watching so closely? You want to ensure your child is a strong and skilled swimmer.

As the Financial Lifeguard, my job isn't just to get people to safety so they can catch their breath; most importantly it's to teach them how to "swim." I don't want my financial coaching clients to need me forever. I have no desire to drag them around the "pool," month after month, doing their budgets for them. My goal is to teach them to be proficient "swimmers" so I can go and rescue someone else who's drowning. Yes, my coaching clients may return to me occasionally when their financial waters take an unexpected rough turn. The end goal is to get my clients to the point of building good financial skills and habits so they don't need me anymore.

Parents, this should also be your goal for your children. Don't just rescue your kids when they are drowning financially, teach them how to "swim." I've seen a multitude of parents who throw their teenagers and adult children financial lifelines over and over again, with no real consequences for the child. The only thing the child learns is the lifeline is there from mom or dad with no strings attached when they mess up with their money. Which is why they call out for it; demand it even, over and over again.

Parents, I hate to break it to you, but it's as much your fault as it is your child's. It's high time you taught them how to swim, because there will come a time when you are not there to offer the lifeline, and they will drown financially. Part of the parental responsibility is to prepare kids to not only survive but thrive *without you* out in the real world. When you don't teach your children how to swim financially, you're stunting their personal growth and straining your own resources.

At a certain point, when kids are around three or four years old, most parents stop carrying them around everywhere and make them walk for themselves, at least most of the time. What if a parent never did that and had a 10 or 12-year-old who still expected to be carried everywhere? We would say that's ridiculous! The parent would be doing a horrible disservice to the child and would probably have a strained back on top of it. How is it we understand the benefits of teaching a child to walk and to swim, but not to be financially savvy?

~

We face several obstacles when teaching our kids about money. The first obstacle is we may not have good money skills ourselves. If our own confidence about money is shaky it's hard to lead by example. The great news is you're improving yours right now by reading this book! You must become a proficient swimmer before you can teach your kids how to swim. When you learn a new money skill and understand it well enough to teach it to your kids, you reinforce it at a deeper level within yourself.

Second, we need to recognize our rescuer tendencies and write out the negative consequences of them. Some people love to be the hero and rescue others out of their financial messes. It's not a healthy way to meet your need for significance. This is why I want you to literally write out on paper the negatives of "saving" people from themselves. Here are some examples: "If I buy Emily another car after she wrecked hers, she will not learn the value or money or the consequences to her behavior." "If I bail Danny out of his credit card debt, I may not have adequate money in my retirement fund and may have to move in with him in my elder years." "If I continue to allow Jen to live here rent free, she will not learn the value of work or what it really costs to be living independently."

The third obstacle is we've trained our child to be a "drowning victim." Because we have bailed them out time and time again, the child has learned to be helpless. We've taught them through our past behavior that we will always be there to throw them a lifeline and solve their problems for them. We have shielded them from the consequence of their bad behavior, so they never learn to change their ways. You see, allowing your kids to feel the pain of their mistakes, especially when the amounts are small, is actually a good thing. Pain is a sign something is wrong, that something needs to change. If you take the pain away, they will continue on the same destructive path. And what happens when you are not there to throw the lifeline and your child doesn't have any clue how to "swim?" We are doing our children a massive disservice if we don't teach them their behavior has real financial consequences. My Dad has often told me, "You learn the most from the mistakes that cost you the most money."

The next time the lifeline is thrown to your child, there must be some effort on their part to retrieve it. *There must be strings attached to our help which are a little unpleasant.* For example, if your 28-year-old able-bodied son is still living at home, not paying any rent or otherwise contributing to the houschold expenses, then set a timeline for him. He must either move out or begin paying $X in rent to you within 60 or 90 days. The difficult part for you will be sticking to your timeline *no matter what.* It's likely he will test you to see if you are serious, so be expecting it.

THE STORY OF THE BUTTERFLY

A man found a cocoon of a butterfly.
One day a small opening appeared.
He sat and watched the butterfly for several hours
as it struggled to squeeze its body through the tiny hole.
Then it stopped, as if it couldn't go further.
So the man decided to help the butterfly.
He took a pair of scissors and
snipped off the remaining bits of cocoon.
The butterfly emerged easily but
it had a swollen body and shriveled wings.
The man continued to watch it,
expecting that any minute the wings would enlarge
and expand enough to support the body,
Neither happened!
In fact the butterfly spent the rest of its life
crawling around.
It was never able to fly.
What the man in his kindness
and haste did not understand:
The restricting cocoon and the struggle
required by the butterfly to get through the opening
was a way of forcing the fluid from the body
into the wings so that it would be ready
for flight once that was achieved.
Sometimes struggles are exactly
what we need in our lives.
Going through life with no obstacles would cripple us.
We will not be as strong as we could have been
and we would never fly.
~ Author Unknown

The takeaway from the butterfly story is this: our kids need some financial friction and consequence in their lives. This will strengthen their money muscles and ensure they are able to thrive out in the real world. What are the consequences of not teaching your kids how to "swim?" They become like a whirlpool, sucking everyone who gets close enough to them into their black hole of financial need.

ACTION ITEMS

Are you teaching your kids the basics of smart money management? Why or why not? Are you lacking in financial knowledge yourself? Do you enjoy being a rescuer? Have your kids learned to be financially helpless? How can you ensure there are consequences to your kids' future money mistakes?

CHAPTER 55

Real Life Money Lessons

A growing number of public and private schools are conducting classes and courses to teach kids about personal finance, but sometimes they aren't teaching your kids the things *you* want them to learn about money. It's important to be intentional about talking with your kids about money in age-appropriate ways. In doing so, you'll help them build a solid foundation for money management which will support them into adulthood.

You don't have to use a formal money curriculum to introduce your children to money management. Often the most profound lessons we can teach our kids about saving, spending, and giving are interwoven into everyday life. Kids learn more from what parents do than what they say. If you are telling your kids that saving money is important, yet you have to take out a cash advance on your credit card to pay for emergency car repairs, the lesson will go in one ear and out the other. This means they will imitate your money habits, so make sure they are good ones! Talk with your kids in age-appropriate ways about your choices with money.

How early should we start teaching our kids about money? I think you can begin the basics as young as four years old, when they're learning to count coins and paper money. This is a good age to make the connection between work and money. Pay them

213

to do some (not all) of their chores. Have them save up their money and take them to the store to buy a toy. It's best to keep it simple at this age. However, you might be surprised by how much young children are capable of absorbing.

CASE STUDY: THE FOUR-YEAR-OLD LEARNS ABOUT THE STOCK MARKET

My Dad began teaching me about money very early in life. In fact, I remember him explaining the basics of the stock market to me at the tender age of four. I would climb into my Dad's lap at least once a week, squeezing in between him and the Wall Street Journal. He picked one stock for me to follow: a hair dryer company. I would scan through the columns of the WSJ looking for "our stock." In a rudimentary way, my Dad explained to me that when the company performed well, the stock price would go up; but if the company didn't do well, the stock price would drop. Maybe he was hoping I'd grow up to be a financial planner or stockbroker! These lessons fostered an early fascination in me to learn about money and how to make it grow.

Grade school age kids can graduate to a system of three piggy banks or envelopes, one each for giving, saving, and spending. (Dave Ramsey's website has some awesome money tools and educational materials for kids of all ages.) You can decide on how much of their chore money goes into each category. If you haven't already, take your child to the bank with you to open up a savings account. There are plenty of opportunities to teach kids about prices, budgeting, coupons, and sales tax during your weekly trips to the grocery store.

Kids who are in junior high may be earning some money outside of chores by babysitting their siblings, having a lemonade stand, or walking the neighbors' dogs. This is a good time to give them more autonomy in their spending, especially if they have proven themselves to be good little money managers.

By the time your kids get to high school, it's time for their first checking account (*not* a credit card!) Deposit the money you'd normally spend on them for clothing, sports, and entertainment and teach them to manage it themselves. They will spend their money differently this way than if you are just paying for everything. It will reinforce that there is a limit to money, and choices need to be made. Teach them how to balance their checkbook when the monthly statement is available. Your high schooler will likely need "training wheels" the first few months of having a checking account, so stay involved until they get the hang of it. This is the time to discuss things like car payments and insurance, student loans, and credit cards. Trust me; you don't want them to learn how to buy a car from a used car dealer!

CASE STUDY: MONEY MANAGEMENT AT THE GROCERY STORE

Shortly after I turned 16 and got my driver's license, I inherited my Mom's old Ford Taurus along with a new responsibility... weekly grocery shopping. My Mom would give me a set amount of cash each week, along with the grocery list. She encouraged me to find ways to save money by allowing me to keep what was left over for gas and spending money. Taking on this responsibility taught me some valuable money lessons including:

- **Sticking to a budget.** I only had a certain amount of cash to pay for the groceries, so I couldn't go over that amount! I carried around a little calculator as I shopped to ensure I stayed on budget.
- **How much groceries cost.** This can be a real shocker for high school and college aged kids! Groceries are not cheap, and it helped me to appreciate the fact that I didn't have to pay for them myself... yet. Better to have some clue about it before you're out on your own.
- **How to save money using coupons and sales.** Because I was able to keep any leftover money from my grocery trip, I was definitely motivated to find ways to save money by shopping the weekly sales, manager specials, and by utilizing coupons!

- **The importance of meal planning.** Around this time, I also started cooking more dinners for the family. I needed to make sure all of the ingredients for the week's meals were on the shopping list!

Parents, if you have a driving teenager or college kid at home, you may want to try this as well! It will teach them money management skills while taking a time-consuming chore off of your plate.

The bottom line is this: we need to train our children and give them good resources for money management. We can't expect the school system to teach them about personal finance because it's the responsibility of loving parents, grandparents, aunts and uncles to do this. By weaving personal finance lessons into everyday life situations, you will set your kids up for money success in adulthood—which is a big parenting win!

ACTION ITEMS

What real life money situations will you use to teach your kids the basics of personal finance? I highly recommend parents read Smart Money, Smart Kids: Raising the Next Generation to Win with Money by Dave Ramsey and Rachel Cruze, which goes into great detail about teaching kids about money in creative and age-appropriate ways.

PART SIX

The Road Ahead

CHAPTER 56

Not Everyone is Going to be Happy for You

You would think once you decide to take control of your spending and make a plan to demolish your debt that you'd have the full support of your family, friends, and co-workers. However, some people are *not* going to be happy for you and may even subtly, or not-so-subtly, attempt to undermine your financial progress. We're going to discuss why this happens and how to handle it with minimal drama.

You might have experienced this phenomenon in other areas of your life. You get your dream job with twice the pay in another state, or you finally get in shape and lose 25 pounds. You expect the other people in your life to be as elated as you are, yet some of them are downright negative about your positive changes. Why? We could write it off as "Haters gonna hate," but chances are there's something else going on under the surface.

Most people do NOT like change. When we make a positive change financially, we start acting differently. We're spending less and saving more. We may not go out with "the gang" as often because we're choosing to cut some expenses so we can achieve the money goals we've put on our Vision Boards. These changes are certainly positive for us, but can be perceived as negative by others in our lives. Especially if this means we are spending *less time* with them. When we change, others can feel threatened because their world also changes. The natural response is to try to persuade us to return to "the way things were."

Some people may feel like we are judging them because they are not making the positive changes we've chosen. When others see us choosing to go out on the town once a month instead of once a week so we can pay off our student loans, they subconsciously realize they should also be making better money choices. You might hear them say things like, "Oh, you think you're too good to go out with us now." "I'm worried about you; you're being too extreme with your budget." "Live a little! You can't take it with you." And certainly, I'm a believer in having some fun money in your spending plan. But don't cave into pressure to change your Financial Roadmap because of what other people say.

As you move down this path toward becoming financially healthy, think about how your positive choices might be affecting the other people in your life. Should you just write off the haters and ignore them? No, I actually think there is a better way to handle these situations. Let's look at an example.

Let's say you're a woman who is struggling with credit card debt. You and your husband have put together a solid plan to tackle the issue. In the past, you and mom have always spent quality time at the mall shopping together. Now, you're choosing to operate on a cash-only basis for budget categories like clothes, shoes, and eating out. This means you're *not* going to be able to meet your mom at the mall every Saturday for mother-daughter bonding over the sales racks at Macy's. You know you're going to get some backlash from your mom about it if you only choose to meet her at the mall once a month. What do you do?

I would suggest inviting your mom over to your house to have an honest conversation with her. It should go something like this: "Mom, John and I are choosing to spend our money differently now because we have a goal to pay off all of our credit cards. The debt is causing us a lot of stress and we're ready for a change. I would really like your support in this. I'm choosing to go to the mall only once a month instead of every week. What are some other ways we can have our mother-daughter time together besides going to the mall?" If you come to the conversation with some suggestions for free or inexpensive excursions you think your mom would enjoy, even better.

You can use this same formula and apply it to other situations. Here's another example. You and your spouse are part of a couples group that goes out to dinner once a week. You've decided the "dining out" category of your budget needs to be reduced in order to make a good dent in your student loan debt. Rather than going out to dinner with the gang once a week, you let them know you'll only be joining them once a month. You may also propose a monthly potluck dinner at your house to replace one of the other weekly outings. If your group of friends agrees, then you'll see them twice a month and still achieve your money goals. Who knows, maybe some of the couples will be relieved because their budgets could use some breathing room as well.

You may notice in my examples, I recommended reducing the frequency versus cutting out the fun activity altogether. There's no reason you shouldn't have room for some portion controlled fun, especially if it's something you enjoy. Have the honest talk using positive verbiage: "We are choosing to spend our money differently now." Don't say things like, "I can't go out this week, because it's not in the budget." You'll just depress yourself and give the other person ammunition to talk you into spending money you've earmarked for your goals. By focusing on your proactive and positive choice to work toward your goals, you'll keep yourself motivated and you could even inspire the other person to do the same. Ask for your friend or family member's support and discuss some alternative ways to spend time together so you won't derail your financial goals. Most people will get on board and applaud your positive changes.

Unfortunately, some people will not be appeased by this conversation and will continue with their negativity. It's important you stand your ground in a positive manner. Do *not* compromise on your money goals! If you fall into the trap of people pleasing, it will make you broke and miserable. I know, because I've lived it. Keep your eyes on the prize! Seek out support from like-minded people who are already financially healthy. They will be happy to cheer you on to success.

ACTION ITEMS

Is there someone in your life who might not be happy with your new money habits? Decide in advance how you will address this in a positive way. Will you stay committed to your financial roadmap even if they don't approve of it?

CHAPTER 57

Push Beyond Your Money Comfort Zone

Whether we know it or not, we all have a comfort zone when it comes to personal finances. We're used to our current amount of income and a certain balance in our savings account or 401(k). If you have a sudden change in your money—even a very positive one—it can be a shock because it pushes you outside of your comfort zone.

Psychologists have shown that people adapt better to increases in wealth when it comes incrementally instead of all at once. It's not unlike a cold swimming pool on a hot summer day. If you start at the shallow end, and slowly walk into the water, eventually getting deeper and deeper, you're allowing your body to slowly adjust to the change in temperature. If you cannon ball right into the deep end, it's a shock to your system, and you may be tempted to swim straight to the edge of the pool and towel off. We can react the same way to an abrupt change to our money situation.

If you're not mentally prepared to handle a sudden windfall, you run the risk of self-sabotaging in a subconscious attempt to return yourself to your comfort zone. This happens frequently to the recipients of big money such as lottery winners, professional athletes, and those who receive large inheritances. Analysts at

Mint.com report that within five years of retirement, 60% of NBA players and 78% of NFL stars will file for bankruptcy. According to a 2012 Vanderbilt University study, 70% of lottery winners end up bankrupt.

CASE STUDY: "THAT'S TOO MUCH!"

When I worked for my family's business as the Vice President of HR & Accounting (and part owner), the company had a policy for many years of keeping the owners' salaries on the low side. The thought was if the company had a great year, the owners would receive their share of the profits and it would more than make up for the lower-than-average salaries.

One year, my boss, Scott, asked me to do some research to see what salaries in our local area were for the various positions held by the owners. He was thinking of raising the owners' salaries because the company hadn't done so in a long time.

I was a little nervous when I presented my findings, because it would mean a very significant boost to all six of the owners' salaries, including mine. After he looked things over, my boss met with me to discuss the raises to submit for the next payroll. I almost fell off my chair when Scott told me he was going to raise my salary by $25,000 per year. I said, "That's too much!" *I actually argued with him about my big raise!* Why? Because it was outside of my comfort zone. Deep down, I wasn't sure I was worth that much. Guess what? My boss won, and I quickly recovered from the shock and acclimated to my new salary.

~

We can purposely and proactively push our money comfort zones to a higher level. Here are some exercises to do this:

- If you haven't already, create your Financial Vision Board with pictures of the material things you want but cannot yet afford. When you first put the pictures on your board, you might be thinking, "There's no way I'm ever going to get this BMW, vacation to Europe, ski boat, etc...." But by looking at these pictures on a regular basis, they become familiar sights. The more you see it, the more comfortable you become with the idea of having it.

- Place yourself in close proximity to people who are at the level of financial health and wealth you aspire to, especially if it makes you feel a little uncomfortable. What type of hobbies do they have? Where do they vacation? What type of homes do they live in? What vehicles do they drive? Close your eyes and imagine going through a day in their shoes.

- Put yourself in close proximity to the material things you aspire to own. Go on a tour of million dollar homes or rent a luxury or sports car for a week. Maybe you have a friend or family member who belongs to a country club you've always wanted to join. See if the person will take you to play tennis or a round of golf. While you're playing, imagine you are already a member there and how it would feel. Treat yourself (and your spouse!) to a night at a 5-star hotel even for just one night. Soak in the environment and imagine always staying at hotels such as this for travel.

- Find the edge of your comfort zone when it comes to income and money in the bank by completing the **Money Challenge Line** exercise. Using the Money is Emotional workbook or a piece of paper, write down your current monthly or annual income. Now cross it out and write down double that number. Would you feel good making double your income or would you feel a little nervous? If you feel positive about it, cross it out and write down three times your current income. Ask yourself the same question. Continue bumping it up (four times, five times, six times, etc.) until you feel nervous, uneasy, or unsure of your ability to handle that amount of money. When you say to yourself, "That's too much," *you've just discovered your Money Challenge Line.* You can do this same exercise with your 401(k) account, bank balances, and total net worth. Once you find your Money Challenge Line, turn it into an afformation you say daily.

Here are some examples: *Why is my income $10,000 per month? Why is my net worth $7 million dollars? Why do I have $100,000 in my savings account?*

You've likely heard the saying, "If your mind can conceive it and you can believe it, you can achieve it." But the flip side is also true: "If your mind can't conceive it and you don't believe it, you won't achieve it." By intentionally pushing ourselves outside of money comfort zones, we're mentally preparing ourselves to thrive, rather than self-destruct when we reach a higher income or net worth.

ACTION ITEMS

Have you experienced a situation when you sabotaged your own success because it would have put you outside of your money comfort zone? Create your financial vision board, if you haven't already. How are you going to put yourself in close proximity to the things and experiences you want? Complete the Money Challenge Line exercise.

CHAPTER 58

Giving is Good for You

Did you know giving money is good for you, physically, mentally, and spiritually? According to the Cleveland Clinic, the following health benefits are associated with giving: lower blood pressure, increased self-esteem, less depression, lower stress levels, longer life, and greater happiness. In a 2006 study, the National Institutes of Health studied the MRI's of people who gave to various charities. They found that giving stimulates the reward center in the brain, releasing endorphins and creating what is known as the "helper's high." Imagine how the world would change for the better if everyone was addicted to this "helper's high!"

Giving is good for us because it makes us less selfish and places the focus on helping others rather than dwelling on our own problems. It's hard to be mad at your jerk of a boss while serving dinner at a homeless shelter to people who are smiling at you, thankful to be eating a hot meal. It's hard to be sad because your friend didn't invite you to the party when you're at the toy store shopping for a child who wouldn't have any Christmas presents without your generosity.

Giving is good for us because it causes us to be grateful for all of the blessings we have. Several years ago, on the weekend before Thanksgiving, I helped with a hot food giveaway for the homeless in the inner city, less than ten miles from my home. In addition to the meal, we also gave out care packages of socks, toiletries, hats, and gloves. Afterward, I cried the whole way home in my car, grateful to God I owned a car and a home with heat and so many other things these homeless people did not. In our consumer-driven society, it's easy to get sucked into the cycle of wanting more and better stuff. Giving to others helps us take a step back and realize how blessed we already are.

Giving is good for us financially because we reap what we sow. Whether you call it Karma or God or the Great Spirit, there is a universal law of sowing and reaping. I can't overstate the importance of giving as part of a healthy financial plan. *Rich Dad, Poor Dad* author Robert Kiyosaki says, "I always chuckle when I hear a person say, 'I'll give money when I have money.' From my point of view, the reason they do not have money is because they do not give money." This is why I tell my coaching clients they need to include giving in their budgets, even if they are in debt. Giving starts the receiving process!

When my Dad helped me with my first budget after I'd crashed and burned, he insisted I give some money to others. I argued with him that *I* was the one who needed a handout! He said, "When you're feeling sorry for yourself, just remember there's someone worse off than you who would love to be in your shoes." I felt like a failure because I had messed up my money situation and had to move back in with my parents for a few months. Yes, it was a setback, but it wasn't the end of the world.

My Dad reminded me I had a roof over my head, food on the table, a good job, and a family who loved me. He suggested I begin my adventures with sowing and reaping by donating just $5 a week to the local homeless shelter, Fairhaven Rescue Mission. Every time I wrote out the check to Fairhaven, I would thank God that I had food, shelter, and clothing. Shortly after I committed to giving $5 a week (and bumping it up as my money situation improved,) wonderful "coincidences" started happening. A creditor was willing to settle for less to wipe out a debt. I received a raise at work despite my annual review being months away. It was like God showing me if I would help others financially, He would step in and help me.

As my finances improved, I gradually increased my giving to at least 10% of my income. I still give money monthly to the homeless shelter, in addition to my church and other charities close to my heart. I treat these donations like any other bill to be paid. And when I feel like I can't afford to part with the money, that's when I know I really need to invest it in others who are less fortunate than me.

Look, I'm not sure exactly how or why the universal law of sowing and reaping works. I just know it does! This is why I make giving a part of my financial plan every month, not just during the holiday season. I encourage you to do the same and see if you are not enriched by the spirit of giving, in your health, in your wallet, and in your heart.

ACTION ITEMS

Do you give to your church or other charities on a regular basis? Which benefits of generosity have you experienced because of it? If you're not giving now, decide which charity you will begin to bless with your next paycheck, even if it's just five or ten dollars.

CHAPTER 59

You Are Rich

You are rich! Don't believe me? If you live anywhere in North America, you are fortunate enough to be in the top 10% of the world's wealth. You may not feel like you're rich if you're not driving a BMW or a Mercedes Benz. You don't belong to a country club or own a yacht. Yet, you are still rich.

- Do you have clean drinking water?
- Are you able to take a hot shower?
- Do you have food in your pantry and refrigerator?
- Do you own a car?
- Do you own a house?
- Do you sleep on a mattress?
- Do you make more than $2.00 per day?

If you answered yes to most or all of these questions, you are indeed richer than 90% of the world. We often forget how good we really have it. We watch celebrity reality shows and think our lives would somehow be better if we had an indoor swimming pool, a bowling alley, and a six-car garage. We forget to be grateful for the many financial blessings already in our possession. There's nothing wrong with wanting to do better financially, but *if we fail to practice gratitude we will never be happy with what we have, no matter how much it is.*

Let's say you have two children, Joey and Emma. Joey never says thank you for anything you provide him. He never says thank you for the meals, toys, clothes and other things you give him on a regular basis. He throws his clothes on the floor and frequently mishandles and breaks his toys with no remorse. Emma, on the other hand, thanks you every night for making her dinner. She puts her dirty clothes in the hamper and her clean clothes in her dresser. She takes good care of her dolls and toys, and generally cleans up after herself. Which child is going to attract more blessings in his or her life? Although you love both Joey and Emma, you might be inclined to bless Emma more because of her attitude of gratitude.

Being grateful for what you have opens the door to countless financial blessings. Being grateful for what we already have creates a sense of peace and satisfaction deep inside of us. It's okay to want more, just ensure you're grateful for what you already have.

ACTION ITEM

Make a daily practice of writing down at least five things you're grateful for each day.

CHAPTER 60

Be Your Own Best Friend

D o you remember the story I told you at the beginning of this book about my best friend Nicholle and her loser boyfriend, Ben? In case you forgot, here it is again:

The year was 1998. My best friend, Nicholle, came to me with a dilemma. Here's what she said, "Christine… my boyfriend, Ben, is in jail because of a DUI. He called me collect and said he's going to go crazy if I don't post bail for him and get him out of there. The problem is I'm living paycheck to paycheck and don't have the money to do it. The only possible way I can bail him out is if I cash in the stock certificates my dad bought me for my 21st birthday. Do you think I should do it? Ben's really pressuring me."

My response went something like this, "Are you crazy? Of course not! Don't you dare cash in those stocks your dad bought you for your birthday! Ben's in jail because he chose to be stupid and drive drunk. He's lucky he didn't kill somebody! Ben's getting what he deserves; let him rot in jail for all I care."

I have a confession to make… The above story isn't *exactly* true. It wasn't Nicholle's boyfriend who was in jail; it was mine.

At a posh restaurant overlooking the skyline of Cincinnati in December of 1994, my Dad presented me with 21 shares of stock of the bank I was working for at the time. It was a very cool and thoughtful 21st birthday gift. I remember thinking it would be a great seed to my financial nest egg that would surely flourish as time passed.

Fast forward two and half years later... Jeff didn't come home after a night of partying, driving my car. I received a collect call from the county jail to find out he'd received a DUI and my car was impounded. Because of Jeff's spotty work habits, I had no savings and was going to have to pay some bills late in order to get my car back. I definitely had no money to post his bail. Jeff insisted I "do whatever it takes" to get him out of there. The only assets I had were those stock certificates my dad had given me for my birthday. My only choice was to cash those in so I could post Jeff's bail, right? People are more important than money, I reasoned. If it were me, I'd want him to do the same for me.

However, it *wouldn't* be me in jail! As a teenager, I never even snuck out of my house for fear my parents would be disappointed in me if they ever found out. I'm a responsible person down deep into my core. But I reasoned with myself that bailing Jeff out was the right thing to do. Why? Because emotion caused me to do stupid things with my money.

Is there a way to pull the plug on these erratic emotions when it comes to making decisions about our money? Yes! I call it the "Be Your Own Best Friend" method. In the two opening paragraphs of this chapter, I restated my dilemma as if it was happening to my best friend, Nicholle. If you go back and look at my response, there's nothing wishy-washy about it. My reaction is swift and visceral. There is no way Nicholle should pay for Ben's mistakes.

If you are grappling with a money situation that is emotionally charged, write out the facts of the situation as if it's happening to your best friend. Write out names and details. Then write down what advice you would give your friend. Guess what? *Each of us should be our own very best friend.* Then be smart enough to take your own advice.

What might have happened if I kept my stock certificates and let Jeff deal with the consequences of his DUI, instead of shouldering them myself? Maybe he would have learned his lesson and decided to be more responsible. Maybe he wouldn't have been convicted of a second DUI six months later…

It can be hard for us to recognize when the people we love are violating our healthy money boundaries. Growing up we hear things like, "The love of money is the root of evil," and "people are more important than money." Be aware that people may use statements like these to guilt us into doing what they want. You are not a bad person for standing up for yourself and erecting healthy money boundaries in your life. You are not responsible for the financial consequences of other people's actions.

You can also use the "Be Your Own Best Friend" method for less dramatic money decisions. What if you're considering purchasing a newer vehicle and you're not sure if it's the right move or not? Simply write out the pros and cons of the situation as if your best friend is pondering the same decision. What questions might you ask of your best friend in this situation? "How many miles does your current car have on the odometer? Does it need major repairs? Do you have cash saved up for the newer car you're looking to buy?" It's easier to frame purchase decisions this way because it takes the emotion out of it. If you see the red convertible you've always wanted at the car dealership, your heart can hijack your wallet before you even know what happened! Back away from the convertible, take a deep breath, and find someplace quiet where you can objectively evaluate the money decision you're about to make.

ACTION ITEM

Are you currently wrestling with a sticky money dilemma? Apply the "Be Your Own Best Friend" method to your situation. Write out the details as if it was happening to your best friend. What advice would you give him or her?

CHAPTER 61

Let It Go

Are you holding onto resentment or anger over a past money situation? Maybe your college roommate stole money from you. Maybe you lent your sister $1,000 two years ago and she still hasn't paid you back. Maybe your workaholic father put making money first instead of spending time with the family. Maybe you're still beating yourself up over past money mistakes you made, as I was, until just recently.

During the early stages of writing this book, I found myself becoming very emotional as I wrote out my money stories on the page. I was surprised at how strong some of my reactions were as I remembered the details of these situations. At first I thought I might be harboring some resentment toward Jeff, and maybe I hadn't completely forgiven him. Later, it hit me like a ton of bricks. The person I most needed to forgive was *me*. I was internally cringing when I retold certain stories about my past, still feeling regret over them, almost two decades later.

I decided to write a letter to my younger self, forgiving her once and for all for the mistakes, both financial and relational, she made during that seven-year period. I found several pictures of myself from that time, and I imagined I was talking to "younger me" as I wrote the letter. Below is an excerpt from it.

Dear Christine,

The reason I'm writing this letter to let you know once and for all, I forgive you. I forgive you for all the stupid decisions you made with money because of emotion. I know you were trying to put love before money and you didn't understand healthy boundaries and the importance of caring for and respecting yourself, which includes your finances.

I know you loved Jeff and you wanted to help him. You saw the potential in Jeff, the best version of himself he could be, if only he really wanted it. As time went on, your relationship became more lopsided and increasingly codependent. You began to go against what you knew was right deep down inside to keep the peace. You always hated conflict and eventually caved into Jeff's wishes so the fighting would stop. Every time you did that, you dimmed your light just a little bit more.

I forgive you for selling your Fifth Third Bank stock, a gift from Dad, to come up with Jeff's bail money. Although Dad has never said it, I feel like this really hurt his feelings by taking this gift and essentially throwing it away. This is the money mistake—although not the biggest one according to the dollars—that was the most grievous. It certainly wasn't the only emotional money mistake you made.

Some of the other memorable ones include: purposely bouncing checks to buy groceries, numerous visits to payday lenders, allowing Jeff to drive my car and the resulting repair bills, credit cards and consolidation loans taken out, and pawning my grandmother's rings to bail Jeff's friend out of jail. Thankfully those rings were recovered. For all of those things and more, I forgive you.

As I look back at pictures of you, I realize you were having a rough time adjusting to Mom and Dad's divorce. You wanted to believe true love still existed and people would fight for each other to stay together. You were trying to prove you were better than your parents, that you wouldn't give up, and love was more important than money. Your loyalty and stubbornness were, and still are, both a blessing and a curse.

I forgive you for not knowing when to say "no" and stand up for yourself. The great news is this is no longer a problem for you! And none of these past experiences have been wasted. You're now teaching and coaching other people to become financially healthy and to make wise, rational decisions in the face of emotional money situations. God has not wasted your pain. He has turned it into something beautiful to help others heal from their financial wounds. God has also brought you into this relationship with your wonderful husband, Nick. He is a good man, providing for you financially and emotionally. Nick loves and appreciates your love and your light, and never tries to quench it.

I forgive you for not leaving Jeff sooner. Although it caused more pain in the short term, it all worked out in the long run. If you had left sooner, you might not have met and started dating Nick. You also might not have some of the stories—painful as they are—that really connect with your coaching clients.

Once and for all, I forgive you, Christine. Without your experiences, I wouldn't be the confident, brave Financial Lifeguard and author who I am today. I love you and I wouldn't change a thing.

Love,
Your Older "Sister," Christine

Do you need to write a letter like this to yourself or to someone else who caused you pain around a money issue? I strongly encourage you to do so. After I wrote this letter to my younger self, I felt like a huge weight of guilt and shame had been lifted from my shoulders. If you're writing a letter to someone else who hurt you, *don't* send it to them. This letter is for you, not for them. This emotional baggage has been weighing you down on your journey to financial health. Write the letter, read it out loud, then burn it or shred it. You don't need that heavy burden anymore. Let it go.

ACTION ITEM

To whom do you need to write a letter of forgiveness: yourself, a family member, or a (former) friend? Set 30 minutes aside today or tomorrow to write that letter and leave the burden behind on the page. (Keep a box of tissues handy, just in case.)

CHAPTER 62

Money is Emotional

'm going to tell you the story of my clients—Doug and Joanne Smith—and their emotional journey from anxiety and embarrassment to confidence and hope. I want you to see a concrete example of how this couple gained mastery over their emotions and their money. By applying many of the Mindful Money Management techniques I've discussed throughout this book, Doug and Joanne were able to work through their negative emotions, and harness the power of the positive emotions to propel them toward their Preferred Financial Future. We are going to dive deep into some of the emotions that surfaced before, during, and after their journey to financial health.

Here is Doug's story, in his own words:

Even though we had a household income in the $100,000 a year range, our debt kept growing, and a career switch that didn't go as planned put us in a big financial hole. Our half-hearted effort at a budget and fiscal responsibility reached a breaking point in November of 2014 when our credit card debt was over $20,000 (plus a mortgage and car payment) and Christmas was only weeks away.

I knew Christine through BNI (my weekly networking group) and decided it was time to finally do the right thing. Putting all of your financial cards on the table and admitting you've been an idiot with your money is not easy. There were tears shed in our initial meeting with Christine as we faced our embarrassment, but we left the meeting with a new confidence and a blueprint for success.

We've followed Christine's blueprint, and we went from $20,000+ in credit card debt to $0 in eight months. There have been a few bumps in the road, as you don't get into debt overnight and you don't get out of it overnight, but with Christine's help we were able to get back on course. I've received some bonuses at work during these eight months. In the past we would have spent the money on something we did not need, but we stuck with our plan and used the money to pay down the debt, add to our emergency fund, and enjoy some quality family time.

Swallowing your pride and admitting you need help is the hardest part of getting out of debt, but once you make that decision the emptiness you feel is quickly replaced with hope.

Doug first talks about half-hearted attempts at budgeting. When we neglect to do something we know we should be doing, this creates an underlying feeling of tension and anxiety. This spills over into our relationship with our spouse or partner and can cause money disagreements and finger-pointing. If you are experiencing these feelings, it's a sure sign you need to do something about it. There are plenty of options out there, including financial coaching, signing up for a money management class, or reading a book on personal finance.

The next thing mentioned is "Christmas was only weeks away." Holidays are stressful enough without adding financial issues to the mix. The Smiths were upset because there was no way they were going to be able to do their normal Christmas spending on their kids and relatives. They felt ashamed and guilty because their money habits were going to negatively impact their kids. The interesting thing is the Smiths told me it ended up being their best Christmas ever, because they were more focused on family time and less distracted by huge piles of presents. But it is important to acknowledge that holidays and other family situations can influence both our emotions and our actions around money.

During Doug and Joanne's coaching session, there were tears shed, and honestly that's not uncommon. I always have a box of tissues at my desk! The Smiths did have some embarrassment over their situation, but I reassured them the only way to get to a better place is to squarely face the truth of their finances. And anyone who has come to me for coaching will tell you, I do not judge others for their financial messes. I've made plenty of my own! My job is always to help people, not judge them.

Shame and embarrassment are the biggest barriers to people admitting they need help with their money. No one wants to admit they have messed up. Money is the final taboo topic in today's society. People would rather discuss their sex lives than their salaries! But it is important to talk about money and money issues, especially when you are struggling.

I love that Doug says they left the meeting with a newfound confidence. How did the Smiths go from anxiety and embarrassment to confidence and hope in the course of a 90-minute coaching session? First, they allowed me to examine all of their financial details objectively and make recommendations. Second, I helped them formulate a budget to meet their specific goals. Finally, I gave them action items to work which started moving them in the right direction.

It's very hard for us to evaluate our own financial messes objectively. I know this from personal experience. When I hit financial rock bottom, my Dad helped me through the budgeting process. It's not that I didn't know how to do a budget—I had an accounting degree! But I could not look at my bills without being upset because Jeff had helped me run them up, however he wasn't going to help me pay them off. My Dad could see things objectively, whereas I was paralyzed by my emotions. Most of my coaching clients are in the same frame of mind when they first come to my office.

The final emotion we see here is hope fueled by accomplishment. I can only encourage my coaching clients and point them in the right direction. This is where the rubber meets the road. The Smiths had to take the financial roadmap we designed together and start taking the steps outlined on it. Doug even says, "There have been a few bumps in the road, as you don't get into debt overnight and you don't get out of it overnight, but with Christine's help we were able to get back on course."

No one does this money thing perfectly—nope, not even me! With every step the Smiths took in the right direction, it resulted in accomplishments which motivated them to keep going. In our follow-up sessions, we would make some tweaks and corrections to make sure the Smiths were staying on course.

The fact that Doug and Joanne went from embarrassment about their finances to practically shouting from the rooftops about their money success in less than a year just has me bursting with pride! Yes, I helped to point the way, but they had to walk in it. Paying off $20,000 in credit card debt is the icing on the cake. It's hard to put a dollar value on the feeling of financial peace of mind.

Yes, you do have to wade through those negative emotions and swallow your pride to face the truth about your financial messes. However, hope and purpose will follow quickly if you choose to get on the path to financial responsibility. Is it worth it? I think the Smiths would tell you a resounding *yes!*

ACTION ITEMS

Are you ready to begin the journey to your Preferred Financial Destination? Write out what your financial life will look like one year from now.

CHAPTER 63

Money Isn't Everything

We've spent our journey together talking about money and how to become and stay financially healthy. Now I have the nerve to tell you, "Money isn't everything." Well, it's not. In fact, it's not money you want at all. It's what money and being financially healthy can do *for* you. Think about it: it's not the dollar bills or the ones and zeroes in your checking account, it's what they represent. Money represents security and peace of mind, the freedom to quit a job that sucks the life out of us, the adventures we can have with our loved ones, the education we can purchase for our children, and the things we buy which bring comfort and value to our lives.

There's a rule I live my life by, and I hope you'll adopt it as well: *People first, then money.* Your relationships should always be your number one priority over making more money. Yes, there is a balance because if you don't work and make a living, your family could end up homeless and hungry... and we certainly don't want that! However, I see so many middle and upper class families running themselves ragged trying to earn *just a little more money* to buy more and better "stuff", and they have almost zero time to spend with their family and friends. And the little time they do have to spend with their family, they are tired, stressed out, and cranky.

Most of us know a close friend or family member who has received a terrible heath diagnoses or tragically died in an accident. It's an alarming wake up call to pay attention to what really matters: our relationships with our loved ones. I definitely want you to give your personal finances adequate attention. Do your monthly budget, pay down debt, contribute regularly to your savings and investment accounts, and seek ways to increase your income. Just don't become obsessed with money and what it can buy. Because the most important thing in life, money can't buy, and that's good quality relationships with the people you love.

CONCLUSION

If there is one thing I want you to take away from reading this book, it's this: *paying attention to your thoughts, words, emotions and behaviors around money pays positive dividends.* Mindful Money Management is about being intentional about your financial life. It does require a small investment of your time and energy to achieve and maintain financial health, but the payoff is less stress, worry, and strife.

Keep in mind no one does this money thing perfectly. We all stumble and fall, so extend yourself a little grace. Those who reach their Preferred Financial Destination are the ones who get back up when they fall and continue down the road. When you find yourself struggling around a certain money issue, come back to that particular chapter or section. Consider this book to be a compass you consult for direction when you're feeling financially lost.

Now that you have finished reading this book, I encourage you to take the time to complete the exercises and answer the questions at the end of each chapter if you haven't already. You can download the free companion workbook at MoneyIsEmotional.com.

My God-given mission is to help as many people as possible become financially healthy. My final ask of you is this: if you gained some nugget of truth that has brought you closer to financial health, share it with others. Give this book as a gift to the person who you know needs it. Share your favorite quote or concept on social media (hashtag: #MoneyIsEmotional). Facilitate a small group book study at your home, church, or workplace. (Download the free small group facilitator's guide at MoneyIsEmotional.com) And please, let me know how the Money Is Emotional book has impacted you by emailing me at Christine@Christineluken.com Here's to your continued financial health!

ABOUT THE AUTHOR

Christine Luken, The Financial Lifeguard, is a Certified Financial Coach, speaker, and writer. She graduated from Northern Kentucky University with a Bachelor's degree in Accounting, with minors in Business Administration and Psychology. Christine worked for 13 years as the Vice President of HR & Accounting in the manufacturing sector before starting her own company, 7 Pillars, LLC in 2010. Prior to that, Christine worked for almost five years in the banking industry, both in retail and collections. She has over twelve year of financial counseling experience, both with individuals and small business owners. Christine teaches Financial Wellness classes to businesses and the public in the Cincinnati area. She is an active member of the Financial Therapy Association and a Kentucky Colonel.

Christine lives in the Greater Cincinnati area with her husband, Nick, and her two cats, Peanut and Little Tiny. She loves to read, golf, paint, swim, and travel to tropical locations.

Recommended Reading

I hope you will view this book as the *beginning* of your financial education, not the end. Here are the books I recommend you add to your library.

Wired for Wealth: Change the Money Mindsets that Keep You Trapped and Unleash Your Wealth Potential by Brad Klontz and Ted Klontz

The Power of Habit: Why We Do What We Do in Life and Business by Charles Duhigg

The Great Little Book of Afformations by Noah St. John

Happy Money: The Science of Happier Spending by Elizabeth Dunn and Michael Norton

The Sudden Wealth Solution: 12 Principles to Transform Sudden Wealth into Lasting Wealth by Robert Pagliarini

College Entrance Game Plan: Your Comprehensive Guide to Collecting, Organizing and Funding College by Dan Bisig and Ryan Clark

Retire Inspired: It's Not an Age; It's a Financial Number by Chris Hogan

Money: Master the Game (7 Steps to Financial Freedom) by Tony Robbins

Get Financially Naked: How to Talk Money with your Honey by Manisha Thakor and Sharon Kedar

Boundaries: When to Say Yes, How to Say No to Take Control of Your Life by Dr. Henry Cloud and Dr. John Townsend

Smart Money, Smart Kids: Raising the Next Generation to Win with Money by Dave Ramsey and Rachel Cruze

ADDITIONAL RESOURCES

For Information on Coaching with the Financial Lifeguard:
http://christineluken.com/financiallifeguard/

To Bring Christine Luken to Speak to your Group or Company:
http://christineluken.com/contact/

Download the free Money is Emotional Companion Workbook:
www.MoneyIsEmotional.com

Download the Financial Coaching Budget Worksheets:
http://christineluken.com/financiallifeguard/

Articles, Videos, and Podcast on the Basics of Money Management:
http://christineluken.com/blog

To Find a Therapist Who Specializes in Money Issues:
http://www.financialtherapyassociation.org/

Article for Entrepreneurs and Small Business Owners:
https://www.linkedin.com/in/financiallifeguard

Investment Calculator:
https://www.daveramsey.com/blog/investing-calculator/

Tips for Getting out of the "Upside Down Car:"
http://www.kbb.com/car-advice/articles/upside_down-on-a-loan/

Compare On-Campus versus Off-Campus Living Costs:
http://www.calcxml.com/calculators/living-on-or-off-campus?skn=124

Mortgage Calculator:
http://www.bankrate.com/calculators/mortgages/mortgage-calculator.aspx

Obtain Your Free Credit Report:
http://AnnualCreditReport.com

Understanding Your FICO Score:
https://www.myfico.com/Downloads/Files/myFICO_UYFS_Booklet.pdf

Age Yourself to Envision "Elder You:"
www.In20Years.com or
www.FaceRetirement.MerrillEdge.com

6-Week Reading Plan

Below is a suggested 6-week reading plan for *Money is Emotional: Prevent Your Heart from Hijacking Your Wallet*. If you are reading this as part of a group study, be sure to read Week One's assigned chapters before your first meeting.

Week One: Introduction & The Battle for Your Money Begins in Your Mind

Day One: Introduction & Thoughts, Words, Emotions (ch.1)
Day Two: Money Stories (ch.2) & Money is Not Evil (ch.3)
Day Three: Your Relationship with Money (ch.4)
Day Four: Money Victim or Victor (ch.5)
Day Five: The Willpower Myth (ch.6)
Day Six: The Dream Session (ch.7)
Day Seven: Your Journey Begins (ch.8)

Week Two: The Budget—Your Key to Financial Health

Day One: Taming the Money Monster (ch.9) & The Reality Check (ch.10)
Day Two: A Budget is Not a Diet (ch.11) & No Cookie Cutter Budgets (ch.12)
Day Three: More Bills Than Money (ch.13) & Mindful vs. Mindless Spending (ch.14)
Day Four: When Is It Okay to Splurge? (ch.15) & The Income Rollercoaster (ch.16)

WEEK FIVE: LOVE & MONEY

Day One: Money and Relationships (ch.47)
Day Two: Get Financially Naked (ch.48) & His Money, Her Money, Our Money (ch.49)
Day Three: Engaging the Uninvolved Spouse (ch.50)
Day Four: Are You a Financial Enabler? (ch.51)
Day Five: The Perils of Cosigning a Loan (ch.52)
Day Six: What's a Few Bucks Between Friends (ch.53)
Day Seven: Parents, Teach Your Children to Swim (ch.54) & Real Life Money Lessons (ch.55)

WEEK SIX: THE ROAD AHEAD

Day One: Not Everyone is Going to Be Happy for You (ch.56)
Day Two: Push Beyond Your Money Comfort Zone (ch.57)
Day Three: Giving Is Good For You (ch.58) & You Are Rich (ch.59)
Day Four: Be Your Own Best Friend (ch.60)
Day Five: Let It Go (ch.61)
Day Six: Money Is Emotional (ch.62)
Day Seven: Money isn't Everything (ch.63) & Conclusion

www.ingramcontent.com/pod-product-compliance
Lightning Source LLC
Chambersburg PA
CBHW021138090426
42740CB00008B/828